What Are Human Rights?

WHAT ARE HUMAN RIGHTS?

BY

Maurice Cranston

Preface by *Reinhold Niebuhr*

BASIC BOOKS, Inc., *Publishers*

NEW YORK

© Ampersand Ltd., 1962
Library of Congress Catalog Card Number 63–12842
Manufactured in the United States of America
Designed by Vincent Torre

Preface

BY REINHOLD NIEBUHR

This small volume by the distinguished English political philosopher, Maurice Cranston, is a lucid, fair, and thoughtful study of the Universal Declaration of Human Rights, which was first adopted in 1948 by the Human Rights Commission of the United Nations. It clears up the confusions—many of them particularly prevalent in America—about the importance and the nature of that declaration.

But Mr. Cranston's study is also a very important contribution to legal and moral theory, far beyond its immediate purpose. For, in the process of clarifying the exact nature of the "human rights" about which the United Nations Declaration speaks, he gives a most cogent analysis of the difference between such universal "rights" and the "rights" bestowed by "positive law"—defined as the specific and enforceable enactments of historic political communities.

WHAT ARE HUMAN RIGHTS?

Mr. Cranston accurately locates the UN's "rights" within the category of "Natural Rights," as defined by John Locke in the seventeenth century and elaborated in our own Declaration of Independence and in the French Revolution's Declaration of the Rights of Man. He further clarifies many confusions by depicting the historical connection between these modern, liberal, democratic conceptions of Natural Rights and the older "Natural Law" theory which Western civilization inherited from Graeco-Roman culture. Natural Law was most specifically defined by the Stoics, but it had been given an earlier definition in Sophocles' *Antigone*, in which the heroine defies the king by appealing to a "higher law" than the positive law of the state: "Nor did I deem that thou, mortal man, couldst by a breath, annul and override the unwritten immutable laws of heaven; which were not born today or yesterday; they die not, and none knoweth whence they sprang."

Cranston's discrimination in dealing with the classical Natural Law conception and the more modern, individualistic Natural Rights conceptions on the one hand, and with the moral relativism of modern "legal positivism" on the other—this latter asserting that the only significant norms are those defined by the "positive law"—makes a genuine contribution to moral and legal theory of the greatest importance, particularly in this country. The importance is due to the fact that he affirms, and establishes by cogent

Preface

arguments, that one need not flee to classical Natural Law theories in order to refute legal positivism.

His own alternative is implicit in his conviction that conceptions of Natural Law and Natural Rights express moral ideals rather than legally enforceable standards, and that these ideals are not less important if an empiricist and historically-minded culture should reveal them to be more relative and less immutable or "self-evident" than their proponents aver. Such ideals affirm the common moral aspirations of a culture, and are "normative," because even historical relativism cannot obscure what is genuinely "human" in these standards. They are relative in the sense that their "self-evidence" derives from the assumptions of a particular culture or age. But they are not arbitrary.

These important discriminations enable Cranston to approach, and to clarify, the confusion that exists in the mind of the public, and in the minds of some idealistic supporters of the United Nations as well, with regard to the Universal Declaration of Human Rights propounded by the Human Rights Commission.

Some of the confusion is due to a lack of understanding of the difference between enforceable "positive law" and the moral and social ideals contained in "Human Rights." Not even the International Court at the Hague can enforce the Human Rights of the Declaration; and the promised "covenant" between the member nations, which was to follow the Declaration, has never become a reality. Some of the confusion, too, is derived from the fact that many of the "rights" are clearly the traditional civil rights of individuals, whereas an amendment of 1952 becomes more collective and speaks of the "right" of a "people" to "self-determination." This Wilsonian (and subsequently Leninist) idea is suspect for many reasons, but particularly because the concept "a people" cannot be defined with adequate clarity. Cranston asks whether Cornwall has the "right" of "self-determination" as against Great Britain. And in the light of recent African history, the question, "Has Katanga the right of self-determination?" is susceptible of no easy or unequivocal answer.

Another source of confusion about the Declaration of Human Rights flows from the fact that these "rights" exist on various levels of moral necessity, political practicability, and economic feasibility. When it comes to "economic and social rights," the Declaration asserts some pretty implausible specimens. In what order of self-evidence shall we put the "right" of the worker "to have a holiday with pay"? It certainly is not in the category of the "right" to vote, or the "right" to trial by jury.

Mr. Cranston is not at all polemical, and he does not denigrate the Human Rights Commission. He merely throws the light of rational discrimination into the dark corners of this current issue and of the whole realm of legal and moral theory. That is why one hopes that this study will receive the widest possible attention.

Contents

	Preface	v
1	What Are Human Rights?	1
2	Rights *and* Morality	13
3	*The* Universal Declaration	29
4	*The* Covenants *of* Human Rights	43
5	Problems *of* Interpretation *and* Enforcement	63
	Appendix	93
	Bibliography	103

What Are Human Rights?

I

What Are Human Rights?

Human rights is a twentieth-century name for what has been traditionally known as Natural Rights or, in a more exhilarating phrase, the Rights of Man. Much has been said about them, and yet one may still be left wondering what they are. John Locke,* the philosopher most often quoted as an authority on the subject, wrote of the rights to life, liberty, and property. The Bill of Rights enacted by the English Parliament

---

* John Locke (1632–1704) wrote *The Letter for Toleration* (1689) and *Two Treatises of Government* (1690) some years before the "Glorious Revolution" in England, but his writings provide the best theoretical justification for what was then accomplished.

after the "Glorious Revolution" in 1689—the same year in which Locke first published his theory of government—named also the right to trial by jury, and prescribed that in all courts of law excessive bail should not be required, nor excessive fines imposed, nor cruel and unusual punishments inflicted.

Locke's reasoning and the example of the English Bill of Rights had a great influence throughout the civilized world. In Virginia in June, 1776, a Bill of Rights was adopted by a representative convention, and its first clause proclaimed "that all men are by nature equally free and independent, and have certain inherent rights, of which, when they enter into a state of society, they cannot, by any compact, deprive or divest their posterity: namely, the enjoyment of life and liberty, with the means of acquiring and possessing property and pursuing and obtaining happiness."

Here the right to happiness is added to those Locke named. The same word recurs in the Declaration of Independence issued by the thirteen American states in July, 1776: "We hold these truths to be self-evident: that all men are created equal; that they are endowed by their Creator with certain inalienable rights; that among these are life, liberty, and the pursuit of happiness."

The United States Constitution of 1789, with concurrent amendments, defined these rights in greater detail. It specified freedom of speech and the press,

What Are Human Rights?

the "right of the people to be secure in their persons, houses, papers, and effects against unreasonable searches and seizures"; the right of an accused person to a "speedy and public trial by an impartial jury of the state"; and the right (which Locke, incidentally, denied to Roman Catholics) to the free exercise of religion. Nineteenth-century amendments made slavery illegal and also stated that "the right of citizens of the United States to vote shall not be denied or abridged by the United States or by any State on account of race, color, or previous condition of servitude."

The Declaration of the Rights of Man and the Citizen issued by the Constituent Assembly in France follows closely the English and American models. It asserts that "men are born and remain free and equal in rights," indeed that "the purpose of all political association is the conservation of the natural and inalienable rights of man: these rights are liberty, property, security, and resistance to oppression." In the same French Declaration liberty is defined as "being unrestrained in doing anything that does not interfere with the liberty of another." Besides property, which is held to be "an inviolable and sacred right," the French Declaration specifies the right to free speech, a free press, religious freedom, and freedom from arbitrary arrest.

Such are the classical statements of the Rights of Man. Yet it would be a mistake to think of this notion as the child of the Enlightenment; it is much more ancient. Citizens of certain Greek states enjoyed such rights as *isogoria*, or equal freedom of speech, and *isonomia*, or equality before the law, which are prominent among the rights claimed in the modern world. In the Hellenistic period which followed the breakdown of the Greek city states, the Stoic philosophers formulated the doctrine of natural rights as something which belonged to all men at all times; these rights were not the particular privileges of citizens of particular states, but something to which every human being everywhere was entitled, in virtue of the simple fact of being human and rational.

Locke was writing as a disciple of the Stoics when he offered his theory of natural rights to seventeenth-century readers who were troubled by the collapse of the traditional political order and forced to think out anew the moral foundations of their own state. The notion of natural rights has since taken deep root in the minds of men. The constitution or the legal codes of practically every state in the world today give at least formal recognition to "the rights of man and the citizen."

Sweden in 1809 and Holland in 1815 followed the English model of incorporating the concept of natural rights into the constitution of a monarchy; other nations copied the American model of a republic having the preservation of men's natural rights as its *raison d'être*. When the United Nations was created after the Second World War, one of the first and most im-

What Are Human Rights?

portant tasks assigned to it was what Winston Churchill called "the enthronement of human rights."

And yet the theory of natural rights has never gone unchallenged, even in the times of its greatest popularity. Among the mandarins of English political philosophy, Hume, Burke, Bentham, Austin, most Idealists of the nineteenth century, and positivists of the twentieth have been opposed to the doctrine. Hegel admitted a concept of rights, but one so transformed that it turned Locke's theory inside out by maintaining that rights belonged not to individuals but to societies or communities. His influence was strong. The Declaration of Rights proclaimed by the nationalist German liberals in 1848 was Hegelian, not Lockian; whereas the American and French declarations had asserted the rights of *man*, the German manifesto spoke instead of "the rights *of the German people*."

Hegel's follower F. H. Bradley wrote in 1894:

> "The rights of the individual are today not worth serious criticism . . . The welfare of the community is the end and is the ultimate standard. And over its members the right of its moral organism is absolute. Its duty and its right is to dispose of these members as it seems best."

Communism no less than nationalism is inclined to this Hegelian conclusion. Marx regarded the notion of the rights of man as a bourgeois illusion; he was opposed to the individualism which underlies the classical doctrine of rights—and by individualism he meant the belief that each particular human person is a unit of value and an end in himself. Marx believed in humanity, in the whole collective mass of mankind, and he argued that this humanity would come into its own when men ceased to think and feel as individuals with separate inalienable rights.

In spite of Marx's teaching on this subject, the Soviet Union, in its constitution of 1936 and again in its revised constitution of 1947, formulated the rights of its citizens on the model of the constitutions of America and France and other bourgeois countries. For example, according to Article 125 of the Soviet Constitution: "The citizens of the U.S.S.R. are guaranteed by law (a) freedom of speech; (b) freedom of the press; (c) freedom of assembly, including the holding of mass meetings; (d) freedom of street processions and demonstrations."

Leaving aside, for the moment, the question of what these "constitutional guarantees" are worth, it is interesting to note that even in the darkest days of Stalinism, the Soviet leaders felt it necessary to give nominal recognition to the notions of rights. The very fact that they have been written into the Communist as well as other constitutions is itself an important sign, for it shows that however obscure the idea of human rights may be, it has somehow acquired almost universal assent.

But let us return to the question with which we

What Are Human Rights?

began. What does it mean to say that all men have rights? Manifestly, the word "right" is ambiguous. First, there is a sense in which to have a right is to have something which is conceded and enforced by the law of the realm. To say that I have a right to leave the country, a right to register as a conscientious objector, a right to bequeath my estate to anyone I choose, is to say that I live under a government which allows me to do these things, and will come to my aid if anyone tries to stop me.

"Right" in this sense is not the same as desert. For example, citizens of some British Commonwealth countries living in England have felt aggrieved because they are not allowed to vote in parliamentary elections in the United Kingdom while citizens of the Irish Republic, which is not even a member of the Commonwealth, have this right. It is a right enjoyed by Irish citizens even if they pay no taxes, and one denied to some Commonwealth citizens, no matter how much tax they pay to the British government, and no matter how long they have lived in the British Isles. From the point of view of deserts, and of justice, there is certainly something odd about a situation where people who both reside permanently in Britain and pay taxes to the British exchequer should be denied a right which is granted to Irish people who commonly repudiate any allegiance to the English throne and do not necessarily pay English taxes. Unjust this may be, but it does not make any difference to the fact that this right *exists*. Irishmen are entitled by English law to vote in English elections. Their right is a verifiable reality.

Rights of this kind I shall speak of henceforth as *positive* rights. What is characteristic of them is that they are recognized by positive law, the actual law of actual states. There is, however, a second sense of the word "right" which is different from positive right, and much closer to the idea of deserts or justice. Suppose the father of a family says, "I have a right to know what is going on in my own house." He is not saying anything about his position under positive law; he is not saying that the courts of justice will ensure that he is kept informed of what happens in his house. He is not so much making a statement of fact as making a special kind of claim. He is appealing to the principle that being the head of a house gives a man a just title to expect to be told what goes on in it. The right he speaks of is a *moral* right.

There is a considerable difference between a right in the sense of a positive right and a right in the sense of a moral right. First, a positive right is necessarily enforceable; if it is not enforced, it cannot be a positive right. A moral right is not necessarily enforceable. Some moral rights are enforced and some are not. To say, for instance, that I have a moral right to receive a decent salary is not to say that I *do* receive one. On the contrary, it is far more likely that the man who says, "I've a right to receive a decent salary" is the man

What Are Human Rights?

who thinks his salary is not what it should be. Immanuel Kant once said that we are most keenly aware of a moral duty when it is at variance with what we wish, or feel inclined, to do. In the same way we are most acutely conscious of a moral right when it is *not* being conceded.

There is a second feature, besides enforcement, which distinguishes moral rights from positive rights. We can find out what our positive rights are by reading the laws that have been enacted, looking up law books, or going to court and asking a judge. There is no similar authority to consult about our moral rights. You may think you have a moral right to something, and someone else may think you have not; but there is nothing you can do to *prove* that you have a moral right, and nothing your critic can do to prove that you have not. What you can do is to try to *justify* your claim, and your critic can try to *justify* his criticisms. But justification is a very different thing from proof.

These considerations point to the first question that must be asked about human rights. Are they some kind of positive right or some kind of moral right, something men actually have or something men ought to have?

Let us take a particular example. According to Article 13 of the Universal Declaration of Human Rights which was "proclaimed" by the United Nations in 1948, "Everyone has the right to leave any country, including his own, and return to his country." If this is read as a statement of fact, it is simply not true.

WHAT ARE HUMAN RIGHTS?

An Englishman, like myself, is assuredly free to leave his country and return to it unless he is detained by order of a court of law. The same situation prevails in many other countries, but not in all. Even in the United States, several American citizens have had their passports impounded by the government since 1948; in South Africa passports are commonly denied to Africans; and behind the Iron Curtain relatively few passports are ever issued at all. Clearly, therefore, the right to leave any country, which the United Nations Declaration says "everyone" has, is not a positive right. Nor, for that matter, has anyone responsible for the United Nations Declaration ever pretended that it was a universal positive right. The intention of the sponsors of that declaration was to specify something that everyone *ought to* have. In other words the rights they named were moral rights.

To say that human rights are moral rights is not to deny that they are positive rights as well for many people. Where human rights are upheld by positive law—where people have what they ought to have—human rights are both moral rights and positive rights. But it is essential to keep in mind the logical distinction between what is and what ought to be, between the empirical and the normative, between the realm of fact and that of morality.

In classifying human rights as moral rights it is

What Are Human Rights?

important to notice something which distinguishes them from other kinds of moral right. This is that they are *universal*. Many of the moral rights that we speak of belong to particular people because they are in particular situations: the rights of a landowner, for example, or the rights of an editor, or a clergyman, or a judge, or a stationmaster. These men's special rights arise from their special positions and are intimately linked with their duties. Human rights differ from these in belonging to all men at all times. They are not rights which derive from a particular station; they are rights which belong to a man simply because he is a man. In the words of Jacques Maritain:

> "The human person possesses rights because of the very fact that it is a person, a whole, master of itself and of its acts, and which consequently is not merely a means to an end, but an end, an end which must be treated as such. The dignity of the human person? The expression means nothing if it does not signify that by virtue of natural law, the human person has the right to be respected, is the subject of rights, possesses rights. These are things which are owed to man because of the very fact that he is man."*

Jacques Maritain writes with eloquence, but whether one can accept his argument or not depends on one's

---

* *The Rights of Man* (1944), p. 37.

attitude to the crucial concept he invokes: that of Natural Law. One cannot speak for long about the rights of man without confronting this notion, for it is customary to say that just as positive rights are rooted in positive law, natural rights—or human rights—are rooted in natural law. The validity of the one depends on the validity of the other. I shall therefore attempt in my next chapter to look a little more closely at the credentials of natural law.

2

Rights *and* Morality

It is a very ancient notion that there is a law which is different from the law of earthly rulers—different from, and also higher and more compelling than, the edicts of courts or princes. One of the earliest and greatest exponents of this thought was Sophocles, who made the conflicting claims of positive law and a higher law the theme of his play *Antigone*.

Readers will remember that Creon, King of Thebes, has decreed that Polynices, a traitor who has been killed in the field, shall be left unburied, his body exposed to the vultures and the dogs. Antigone, the sister of Polynices, rebels against this ruling, because, she claims, every man has a right to burial. "And what right has the King," she demands, "to keep me from my own brother?" Antigone buries the corpse, is discovered, arrested, and taken to Creon.

"Do you know the law?" the King asks her.

"Yes," she replies.

"Then why did you break it?"

Antigone answers that the edict she has disobeyed is not sanctioned by conscience; it may be the law of the state, but it is contrary to the law of justice:

Nor did I deem that thou, a mortal man,
Could'st by a breath annul and override
The immutable, unwritten laws of heaven:
They were not born today nor yesterday;
They die not, and none knoweth whence they sprang.

Creon replies that Polynices was a traitor and that no ruler can let traitors go unpunished. A state must have laws and uphold them. The ruler must be obeyed in all things, just and unjust alike, or the result will be anarchy. "And what evil," Creon asks, "is worse than anarchy?"

Sophocles would not have written as good a play as he did if he had not made the case for Creon as strong, in its way, as he made the case for Antigone. Drama—and history—yield many examples of subjects with far better causes than Antigone's in conflict with rulers with far worse causes than Creon's. The merit of Sophocles' play is that it simplifies nothing. It shows what a serious and terrible thing it is to defy that positive law by which the safety of society is secured, to rebel against established authority in the name of

Rights *and* Morality

conscience or "the immutable, unwritten laws of heaven."

Sophocles, after all, was a statesman and a general as well as a poet. And yet he was clearly on the side of Antigone against Creon. He wrote to win the public's sympathy for what she says and does. Creon argues that "the state must be obeyed in all things—*just and unjust alike.*" Antigone's claim is that the state need not be obeyed if what it commands is unjust. Sophocles is with her. He believes, as she does, that the unwritten law of justice is superior to the law of the state. The rights Antigone claims are rights bestowed by the higher law, so that positive law cannot take them from her.

It is easy to respond emotionally to Sophocles' play, but whether one can accept his argument depends finally on whether one agrees with him that there is a law which is higher than positive law. Is there? And if there is, what is it? Some might be content to say the divine law, the law of God. This may be the best answer, but unfortunately it raises other and no less difficult questions. How do we know God exists? How do we know He lays down moral laws and bestows moral rights? And how do we know what those rights are?

Philosophers and jurists have been reluctant to surrender the whole issue thus to theologians. The most popular answer among philosophers and jurists to the question, "What is the law which is higher than positive law?" has been "natural law." This concept of natural law, though foreshadowed by Sophocles, and to some extent by Aristotle, was first elaborated, together with the concept of natural rights, by the Stoics of the Hellenistic period. Natural law for them embodied those elementary principles of justice which were apparent, they believed, to the "eye of reason" alone. The Stoics of Rome, though jurists rather than philosophers, upheld the same idea. Cicero said, "There is a true law, right reason, in accordance with nature; it is unalterable and eternal."

The political theory of medieval Christendom put even greater stress on natural law, which was identified with the law of God; and after the Renaissance, natural law was restated in secular, modern, individualist terms by Grotius and Pufendorf and Locke.

This is not to say that Cicero and St. Thomas Aquinas and Locke all understood natural law in exactly the same way. I do not, for example, believe that Cicero or St. Thomas thought of natural law as something which bestowed the right of rebellion in the way that some of the Greeks did or that Locke did. Yet the idea of natural law as a universal moral law which transcends the law of states is an idea by which European thinking about political and legal obligation has been permeated for more than two thousand years. And although it went out of fashion in the nineteenth century, it has come into favor again in recent years. At Nuremberg in 1945, natural law was freely invoked

Rights *and* Morality

as the legal basis of at least some of the elements of the indictment of the Nazi leaders.

Natural law is thus a living as well as an ancient idea. It might nevertheless be a fallacious one. There is certainly something suspicious about the things which are said by many champions of natural law. Consider, for example, a remark from the writings of the eighteenth-century jurist William Blackstone: "Natural law is binding all over the globe; no human laws have any validity if contrary to it." Now if the word "valid" means what it commonly means for lawyers, this statement is simply untrue. For by a valid law, lawyers commonly mean a law which is actually upheld and enforced by the courts, a law which is pronounced valid by a duly established judge. A great many laws contrary to natural law were upheld by courts in different parts of the globe in the eighteenth century when Blackstone wrote those words. For instance, there were the laws which authorized slavery, an institution which Blackstone himself regarded as being contrary to natural law. Laws equally antithetical to natural law were upheld by duly constituted courts in Germany at the time of the Third Reich.

Thus, in the usual lawyers' sense of the word "valid," some positive laws which are contrary to natural law *are* valid; if this is what Blackstone was denying, then what he was saying was false.

The truth of the matter, however, is that Blackstone was trying to say something else. He was thinking of a kind of validity which is different from validity in the ordinary legal sense. He meant that any positive law which was contrary to natural law had no validity *in conscience;* he meant that such a law was not *morally* compelling, and had no *just* title to obedience. But Blackstone failed to make this point as he might and should have made it. He failed to discriminate between the empirical and the normative sense of validity, between what is and what ought to be.

Locke is in some ways an even more unsatisfactory exponent of natural law. In his Latin *Essays on the Law of Nature*,* which were discovered and published quite recently, Locke argues that because the study of the universe shows that laws are operating throughout nature it follows that there must be laws governing the conduct of men. Locke does not mean psychological laws; he means moral laws, the sort of laws embodied in natural law. Science, says Locke, shows that laws are universally operative. Therefore, he concludes, science demonstrates the existence of natural law.

This is a bad argument. For the laws discovered in nature by scientists are not laws in the sense in which moralists and lawyers speak of laws. A scientific law is an observed regularity in nature, and it embodies a kind of prediction. It is not something which can be obeyed or disobeyed at will. If something happened which was contrary to an established scientific law,

---

* Edited by W. von Leyden (1952).

Rights *and* Morality

that scientific law would no longer be a scientific law; it would become a discredited, outmoded, forsaken scientific hypothesis. A law of conduct, on the other hand, can be obeyed or disobeyed; and it certainly does not cease to be a moral law if someone breaks it.

Locke's argument is an attempt to derive a conclusion about law in the sense of moral law from a true statement about law in the sense of a scientific law; it rests on an unfortunate mistake of logic. In fairness, however, it must be said that this is not peculiar to Locke. It is a lucid statement of one of the standard traditional arguments for the existence of natural law.

This sort of mistake has prompted some theorists to argue that the whole idea of natural law is a form of bogus metaphysics rooted in confusion of language. Bentham was of this opinion; or perhaps one should say Bentham *is* of this opinion, for his body, embalmed and dressed in the clothes of 1831, still sits in a little cabinet in the hall of University College, London. At any rate, he wrote in *Anarchical Fallacies:* "Right is a child of law; from real laws come real rights, but from imaginary law, from 'laws of nature,' come imaginary rights . . . Natural rights is simple nonsense; natural and imprescriptible rights (an American phrase) rhetorical nonsense, nonsense upon stilts."

Bentham is here stating in picturesque language the central tenet of legal positivism—namely, that only positive law is real law and that natural law is not law at all. Legal theorists since the eighteenth century have tended to attach themselves to one of two schools: the school of natural law or the school of legal positivism. The arguments of positivism have usually been, or have seemed to be, more rigorous than those of the champions of natural law; but it is my belief that they go just as far wrong. There is something arbitrary and dictatorial about the positivist assertion that only positive law is law.

Clearly, natural law is not law in the same sense in which positive law is law. Positive law is a collection of specific enactments, with definite sanctions attached to many. Natural law is not written down and carries no specific sanctions. But this does not mean, as the positivists claim, that it is unreal, imaginary, fallacious, or meaningless. It can be regarded as such only if one insists that all law shall be like positive law. But this demand is intolerably high-handed and dogmatic. The English language allows for a very much freer use of the word "law." Natural law is entitled to the name law because it is *authoritative*, something which can be obeyed or disobeyed. This is not to say that the principles of natural law are in any crude sense imperatives. But neither are the laws contained in positive law. Professor Gilbert Ryle has written (although in another connection):

"Ethical statements, as distinct from particular *ad hominem* behests and reproaches, should be regarded as warrants addressed to any potential givers of behests and reproaches; *i.e.* not as personal action-

Rights *and* Morality

tickets but as impersonal injunction-tickets; not imperatives but 'laws' that only such things as imperatives and punishments can satisfy. Like statute laws they are to be construed not as orders, but as licences to give and enforce orders."*

The chief point I wish to make here is that moral laws are in some respects like positive laws, in other respects unlike them. The differences are extremely important. But the resemblance is important too, and the word "law" is as properly employed in the case of natural law as in the case of positive law. Each kind of law has its own authority: positive law the authority of force, natural law the authority of conscience or morality; and when positive law coincides with natural law it has the authority both of force and of conscience. The test of validity, the criterion of authenticity, is different in each case. The answer to the question, "Is so-and-so a right?" depends, if it is a positive right, on whether it is *enforced*. If it is a natural right or human right which is in question, the answer depends on whether it is demanded by *justice*. Positive law secures the enforcement of positive rights; natural law gives the justice to natural rights.

Bentham's hostility to natural rights and natural law was not only due to his belief that they were unreal metaphysical entities; he also believed—and it was this

---
* *The Concept of Mind* (1949), p. 128.

which made him so impassioned—that talk about natural rights was mischievous. This attitude was shared by certain other critics of natural rights, such as David Hume and Edmund Burke.

This at first seems rather odd, since Bentham's general political outlook was entirely opposed to that of Hume and Burke. The explanation is that they apprehended different kinds of mischief. Bentham, a radical, objected to proclamations of natural rights because he thought that they took the place of ordinary and effective legislation. His argument was that governments which issued declarations of the rights of man were merely making rhetorical utterances which cost them nothing, instead of getting on with the real work of reform. Hume and Burke, on the other hand, were conservatives who disliked talk about the rights of man because it inflamed the common people to revolutionary action. It led men to think they were entitled to have things which they could not possibly have.

Burke in his *Reflections on the Revolution in France* says that the sponsors of the French Declaration of the Rights of Man have done great social harm by proclaiming what he calls the "monstrous fiction" of human equality. Natural differences between men are so great, he argues, that equality is an impossible objective. And to set forth this fiction as if it were a reality is to inspire "false ideas and vain expectations into men destined to travel in the obscure walk of laborious

Rights *and* Morality

life" and "to aggravate and embitter that real inequality which it never can remove."*

I think we must admit that all these criticisms of natural rights have some force in them. There has undoubtedly been a connection, as the conservative critics say, between propaganda for the rights of man and much revolutionary action in the modern world, not only in the case of such successful revolutions as the English Revolution of 1688, the American Revolution, and the Great Revolution in France, but equally in the case of revolutionary movements which have been less favored by fortune. Undoubtedly also, in our own time, which has been characterized by so many revolts against alien rule or colonialism, easy talk about human rights has inspired, in Burke's words, "false ideas and vain expectations" among the inhabitants of many economically backward places.

Bentham's complaint about declarations of metaphysical rights being a wretched substitute for the enactment of positive law has also a close relevance to the problems of the present day. One can well imagine that a Hungarian or a South African who has had his passport impounded by his government might find it particularly irritating to read in the Universal Declaration of Human Rights that "everyone has the right to leave any country, including his own . . ." If he is denied the positive right, of what use is it to him to be

---

* Burke, *Works* (1852), Vol. V, pp. 180–181.

told that he has this human right, this moral right? What he wants is deeds, not words. And that, in the end, is what not only he and Bentham but all of us want. Even so, I think we should not follow Bentham in being so readily contemptuous of words. It *is* of some use to the man who is refused the right to leave his country that the world should formally recognize his moral right to do so. Indeed, such a man can only protest as he does insofar as he can make people understand that a *wrong* is being done to him, that something he ought to have is being denied him. He may dislike being confined within the borders of one republic, but he cannot claim that it is *wrong* that he should be so confined without appealing to some general or universal principle that no man ought to be so confined—without invoking, in other words, the moral right of everyone "to leave any country, including his own."

Bentham's mistake was to pass from the true proposition that natural rights are different from positive rights to the unjustified conclusion that natural rights are nonsense. To speak of morality, of what ought to be, is to make statements which it is very difficult even for professional philosophers to analyze; but it is not to speak of what is meaningless. As for the "mischief" done by talk of the rights of man, we must also remember that harmful social consequences can be attributed to the influence of legal positivism.

Most positivistic jurists, in saying that natural law

Rights *and* Morality

is not law at all, have intended to say no more than that positive law is the only law which it is worth the while of lawyers to think about. However, the dissemination of the idea that positive law is the only law which it is worth the while of lawyers to think about has encouraged the belief that positive law is the only law which it is worth the while of *anyone* to think about. What is worse, it has encouraged the belief that positive law, being the only genuine law, is the only law which should be *obeyed*. The most sensational consequences of this line of thinking were to be observed in Germany under Hitler. There the edicts of the Nazi state were defined and enforced by men who sat on the bench and wore the robes of judges, and the great mass of German people did not doubt that those edicts were lawful, and therefore required obedience. The voice of an Antigone was but seldom heard among them; and this was doubtless in some part due to the influence of positivism in German jurisprudence; for the doctrine of legal positivism is in effect identical with that of Creon, that law is nothing other than the command of a puissant sovereign.

Legal positivism encourages these attitudes, but in fairness one must add that it does not necessarily teach them. The primary objective of legal positivism is to distinguish positive law from morality. In defining law as it does, in making us conscious of what positive law is, legal positivism might also serve to make us more conscious of what morality is. It pushes morality out of the domain of jurisprudence; it says that moral philosophy is no part of the particular professional concern of the lawyer; but it does not deny that it is part of the general concern of ordinary men.

Indeed the legal positivists and the champions of natural law have one great thing in common: they are both inspired by a sense of the great difference that exists between positive law and morality. It is after they have recognized the distinction that they part company, the theorists of natural law maintaining that morality is still part of law, and an essential part, the positivists wishing to remove it from law to the realm of moral philosophy.

Since it is as a political theorist and not as a lawyer that I have presumed to write these pages, I cannot decently quarrel with the positivists about the classification of natural law. Indeed my own work owes as much to the one school as it does to the other. But I believe that the use of the positivistic technique can itself serve to show that the champions of natural law were not so far wrong, after all. For the more one studies the use of the word "law" among English-speaking peoples, the more one comes to realize that morality is, so to speak, built into its meaning. For although we must agree with the positivist that *enforcement* rather than justice is the necessary condition of a positive law being a positive law, one cannot talk for long about law without having entered, perhaps imperceptibly, the realm of value. The word "law" in its

Rights *and* Morality

most frequent uses is a normative word; its definition is intimately linked with the word "justice," which is a normative word in all its uses. The law is defined as a system of justice, and justice, according to the first definition given in the Oxford Dictionary, is "just conduct; fairness; the exercise of authority or power in maintenance of right." This is not to say that all laws are just—far from it; but in looking at law we are looking for justice.

Having recognized the crucial distinction between the empirical and the normative, between the positive and the moral, we have to pass on to a further stage of awareness: that of recognizing how the two are interwoven in the very language that we use. We cannot give a complete account of what we mean by law in terms of facts alone.

3

The Universal Declaration

ONE OF the difficulties which confront the student of human rights in the world today is that of ascertaining how far the nominal "legal rights" specified in the written laws of different states are in fact positive rights. According to the documents, the position is most satisfactory. But if we pass from the study of written constitutions and written law to the actual practice of governments, the story is a very different one. The historic natural rights are positive rights in only a small number of countries.

The missing factor is that principle which the positivists emphasize—enforcement. And how is that to be provided? If particular governments choose not to enforce the rights they nominally concede, what is there to be done about it? If a man is deprived of his rights by his rulers, to whom can he appeal? He cannot appeal to the International Court of Justice at The Hague, because only states are received as litigants there. He cannot appeal to the European Court of Human Rights unless he is a resident of Western Germany or of one of nine small European states.* In many ways the situation of modern man is worse than that of his medieval forebears; for in medieval Christendom the Church both saw itself as the supreme authority on natural law and enjoyed enough power to impose its will on temporal princes. In the modern world, the United Nations is the organization best placed to perform a corresponding function, and I propose in the following pages to consider how far it might reasonably be expected to do so.

The interest of the United Nations in the question of human rights is well known. Article 55 of its Charter stipulates that the United Nations "shall promote respect for, and observance of, human rights and fundamental freedoms"; according to Article 56 "all members pledge themselves to take joint and separate action in cooperation with the Organization for the achievement of the purposes set forth in Article 55."

Two questions immediately arise: (1) What rights

---

* Austria, Belgium, Denmark, Iceland, Ireland, Luxembourg, The Netherlands, Norway, and Sweden.

The Universal Declaration

does the United Nations wish to promote? (2) What has the United Nations done to promote them?

The Commission on Human Rights appointed by the Economic and Social Council of the United Nations held its inaugural meeting in May 1946, when the first of its allotted tasks was to submit to the General Assembly recommendations and reports regarding "An International Bill of Rights." Mrs. Eleanor Roosevelt of the United States was elected chairman of the Commission, and the other countries represented were Nationalist China, France, Lebanon, Australia, Belgium, Byelorussia, Chile, Egypt, India, Panama, the Philippine Republic, the U.S.S.R., the United Kingdom, Uruguay, and Yugoslavia, which was at that time still a member of the Soviet bloc.

The United Kingdom at once put forward a draft Bill of Rights in the form of a convention or treaty which both named the specific human rights to be recognized and provided for international machinery to deal with alleged violations of those rights. The British delegation not unnaturally interpreted the expression "Bill of Rights" as denoting an instrument of positive law, and therefore understood the duty of the Commission to be that of finding a formula for making human rights enforceable, for making them positive rights. In this the British were supported by the Indians, and also by the Australian representative, who put forward detailed proposals for setting up an International Court of Human Rights which would sit in judgment in the case of any alleged violations of the rights as specified in the proposed bill.

The Soviet representative criticized these proposals which emerged from liberal governments of the English-speaking world. He protested that it was "premature" to discuss any measure of a binding or judicial nature. Russia was willing to support a Bill of Rights, but only a "bill" understood as a manifesto of rights. Perhaps, like Bentham, he saw that a mere declaration of rights need cost no one anything. Plainly, since citizens of the Soviet Union already had the nominal "legal right" to free speech and so forth guaranteed by their constitution, the Russians could hardly deny the same nominal rights being acknowledged as universal rights by the United Nations. What the Russians were definitely not going to tolerate was any machinery for enforcement.

The Commission on Human Rights set up by the United Nations had, however, its instructions to obey, its Bill of Rights to draw up. Failing to agree on what a "bill" meant, the commission hit upon a compromise. If it could not produce one document, it would produce two. First there would be a manifesto or declaration "defining in succinct terms the fundamental rights and freedoms of man which, according to Article 55 of the Charter, the United Nations must promote." Later there would be "something more legally binding than

The Universal Declaration

a mere Declaration," and this second instrument it was decided to call a "covenant."

The full text of the Universal Declaration of Human Rights will be found in the Appendix to this book. It is considerably longer than the declarations issued in the Age of Reason, though not necessarily better.

In the early articles of the Universal Declaration the language is that of the old natural rights tradition. The rights to life, liberty, property, equality, justice, and the pursuit of happiness are spelled out in twenty articles, which name, among other things, the right to freedom of movement; the right to own property alone as well as in association with others; the right to marry; the right to equality before the law and to a fair trial if accused of any crime; the right to privacy; the right to religious freedom; the right to free speech and peaceful assembly; the right to asylum. Among the institutions outlawed are slavery, torture, and arbitrary detention.

The Universal Declaration of 1948 did not, however, limit itself to this elaboration of the classical principles. It includes a further set of articles which name rights of another kind. Article 21 states that "everyone has the right to take part in the government of his country"; and further articles affirm the universal right to education; to form trade unions; the right to equal pay for equal work; the right of everyone to "a standard of living adequate for the health and well-being of himself and his family"; and, what is even more novel, the right to rest, leisure, and "periodic holidays with pay."

The difference between these new rights and the traditional natural rights was not unnoticed by those responsible for drafting the Declaration. In the records of the Commission the rights named in the first twenty articles are called "political" or "civil" rights; the further rights are called "economic and social rights." I shall now adopt this terminology. The inclusion of "economic and social rights" in the Universal Declaration represented a considerable diplomatic victory for the Communist members of the United Nations, even though, when it came to the point, they did not actually vote for the Declaration of 1948, but merely abstained, so that it was passed and proclaimed *nemine contradicente* rather than unanimously.

Economic and social rights were unknown to Locke and the natural rights theorists of the eighteenth century, and it may be thought a mark of progress that they should be considered human rights today. But there is a danger here of being misled by good intentions, a danger which, in the history of the United Nations, the Communists have exploited to their own advantage. The language of "rights" is alien to Marx, but it is not difficult to see how it has been grafted on to Marxism by politicians of the twentieth century. What Communism does genuinely care about, and

The Universal Declaration

does in many cases actually offer, is social security, universal education, free health services, guaranteed employment, and other material benefits for the mass of the people. What Communism fails to provide are the things which our countries of the West do offer: freedom, including freedom of speech and movement and assembly; the opportunity of individual development; the enjoyment of private property; security from arbitrary arrest, from secret trials, and from forced labor. And these things which we in the west set such store by are what have been traditionally called men's "rights." What the modern Communists have done is to appropriate the word "rights" for the principles which *they* believe in.

The United Nations Commission was irresolute in the face of this situation. It decided to regard *both* sets of "rights" as equally authentic and to include both in the Universal Declaration. After all, they could tell themselves, everybody believes, ultimately, in economic and social rights *and* in political rights. Different people put a different emphasis; but in the end they are all agreed. Now this, alas, is a slovenly and muddled way of thinking about the subject, and the United Nations is still paying the penalty for it. For a brisk decision to agree on everything made it possible to bring out the Declaration in eighteen months; fourteen years, however, have since elapsed, and the United Nations Assembly has not yet got through the "second stage" of the Bill of Rights, the covenant—or rather the covenants, for the Commission was soon forced to realize that the difference between political rights on the one hand and social and economic rights on the other was such a far-reaching difference that no single "legally binding document" could be made to serve the claims of both; and instead of one draft covenant, the Commission has presented the Assembly with two.

The necessity of this might well have been foreseen; for the truth of the matter is that such a right as the "right to holidays with pay" *cannot* be a right in the sense in which the historic natural rights—the rights, for example, to life and liberty—are rights. The idea of holidays with pay is an attractive one, and, in certain circumstances, a morally compelling one. But a human right has always been understood as something more than this. A human right *by definition is a universal moral right*, something which all men, everywhere, at all times, ought to have, something of which no one may be deprived without a grave affront to justice, something which is owing to every human being simply because he is human.

We have seen that the question, "Is so-and-so a human right?" cannot be answered in the way in which we answer the question, "Is so-and-so a positive right?" But the question can nevertheless be answered. There are still tests for the authenticity of a universal moral right. The first is the test of *practicability*. When Immanuel Kant wrote his celebrated phrase "ought implies can" he meant, among other things, that it is not

The Universal Declaration

a man's duty to do what it is not physically possible for him to do. You cannot reasonably say I ought to have jumped into the river to rescue your drowning child if I was nowhere near the river at the time your child was drowning there. What is true of duties is equally true of rights. It is utterly impossible at present, and it will be for a long time yet, to provide holidays with pay for everybody in the world. For the millions of people who live in those parts of Asia and Africa and South America where industrialization has hardly begun, it is nonsense to talk of a "right to holiday with pay." At best it is a hypothetical right, something they should have if they could have. But because they cannot have it, the so-called universal right to holidays with pay is not a right at all.

The natural rights to life, liberty, and so forth have always been understood as categorical rights, rights nobody could find any excuse for not respecting. Such "political rights" can be readily secured by legislation. The economic and social rights can rarely, if ever, be secured by legislation alone. Moreover, the legislation by which political rights are secured is generally very simple. Since those rights are for the most part rights against government interference with a man's activities, a large part of the legislation needed has to do no more than restrain the government's own executive arm.

Nor is there any difficulty about putting into effect such a principle as the right to trial by jury. This is no longer the case when we turn to the "right to social security," the "right to work," and the rest of the economic and social rights. For a government to provide social security, it needs to do more than make laws; it needs to have access to very great wealth; and most governments in the world today are poor and cannot raise money. The government of India, for example, has earnest progressive ambitions, but it cannot command anything approaching the resources which would be needed to guarantee each one of the 408 million inhabitants of India "a standard of living adequate for the health and well-being of himself and his family," let alone "holidays with pay."

The second test of the authenticity of a universal moral right is the test of *paramount importance*. Here the distinction is less definite, but not less crucial. And here again there is a parallel between rights and duties.

It is a paramount duty to relieve distress, as it is not a paramount duty to give pleasure. It would have been my duty to rescue the drowning child from the river if I had been there; but no one could say that it is my duty, in the same sense, to give expensive birthday presents to the children of my friends. This difference is obscured in utilitarian philosophy, which analyzes moral goodness in terms of the "greatest happiness of the greatest number"; but common sense does not ignore it. Liberality and kindness are reckoned moral virtues; but giving handsome presents is not

The Universal Declaration

morally compelling in the sense that rescuing a drowning child is morally compelling. Holidays with pay are excellent, too; they contribute to the greatest happiness of the greatest number. But they are not a matter of paramount importance, like freedom of speech or equality before the law.

Let us consider a particular case. At the Tenth Assembly of the United Nations, it was reported that "Mr. Himumuine, a Native school principal of South West Africa, has been unable to avail himself of a scholarship at Oxford University because the Union of South Africa has refused him a passport, and has given no reason for its action."*

It is hard for people like myself to read this item without immediately thinking in the language of

---

* UN General Assembly records, Tenth Session, Agenda Item 938. It was possible for the United Nations to receive a petition in this particular case, not because it was a particularly flagrant or unusual case of persecution, but because of the peculiar status in international law of South West Africa. The Union (afterward the Republic) of South Africa was given a mandate over this territory by the League of Nations, and it claims that since the demise of the League it has no international obligation regarding the territory. The UN claims that it has inherited the supervisory responsibility of the League and that South Africa should place South West Africa under UN Trusteeship. The International Court of Justice at The Hague in 1950 upheld the claims of the UN, but South Africa has refused to yield. The UN therefore assumed the right to examine information and petitions relating to South West Africa. See *From Dependence to Freedom*, UN Publications, 61.1.10 (1961).

rights. The government which stopped this African scholar from leaving the country to take up his place at Oxford has, we feel, violated an elementary principle of justice; it has deprived the man of a simple right of movement to which everyone, everywhere, is morally entitled. Here we are confronted with something which belongs to a dimension quite different from any right to holidays with pay. There are certain deeds which should never be done; some freedoms which should never be invaded; some things which are supremely sacred. And it is these sacred things—and nothing so relatively trivial as holidays with pay—which constitute the universal moral rights of all mankind.

If a Declaration of Human Rights is to be what it purports to be, it must be a declaration of universal, paramount, categorical moral rights. To put secondary and hypothetical rights in such a list is not only illogical; it is also likely to bring the whole concept of human rights into disrepute. People may recognize—and it is not difficult to recognize—that the right to holidays with pay is neither paramount nor categorical, and then go on to suppose that none of the other rights named in the Universal Declaration is a categorical or paramount right either. "It would be a splendid thing," people might say, "for everyone to have holidays with pay; a splendid thing for everyone to have equality before the law, and freedom from arbitrary arrest, and freedom of speech and worship.

The Universal Declaration

A splendid thing, and some day perhaps . . ." The effect here is that of pushing all human rights out of the clear realm of the morally compelling into the twilight world of utopian aspiration.

Rights are by such means reduced to ideals. And it cannot be emphasized too often that human rights are not ideals, not utopian aspirations. The men who rebelled against James II in England in 1688, and those who rebelled against George III in America in 1775, had not the slightest thought of introducing a utopian society. They rebelled because their monarchs had started to take away what they regarded as the minimal conditions of a tolerable society. It was not "ideals" that anyone thought of in 1688 or 1775 but the essential minimal rights of man.

Equally, in the Second World War, what united people against Hitler was not that the Germans stood between them and their ultimate aspirations, but that the Germans threatened their most cherished freedoms.

What vitiates the Universal Declaration of Human Rights is precisely that it does not distinguish between rights and ideals, or, rather, that it attempts to be a statement of both at the same time. The essential rights are stated; and in the preamble there is one sentence which reveals a true understanding of what is meant by a human right: "Whereas it is essential, if man is not to be compelled to have recourse, as a last resort, to rebellion against tyranny and oppression, that human rights should be protected by the rule of law . . ." There is no doubt that the meaning of a human right is caught in *that* utterance. On the other hand, it is afterward written: "Now therefore the General Assembly proclaims this Universal Declaration of Human Rights as a common standard of achievement for all peoples and all nations . . ." And however the feeble phrase "a common standard of achievement" is read, its chief effect must be to remove whatever follows from the region of what is immediately and unequivocally compelling into that of distant aspiration.

Hence, if the work of the United Nations for human rights were to be judged on this Declaration alone, it might well be suspected of doing as much harm as good. However, when the General Assembly of the United Nations issued the Declaration in December 1948, it also asked the Commission on Human Rights to prepare "as a matter of priority a draft convention on human rights and draft measures of implementation."* To this other, and longer, story we shall turn in the following chapter.

---

* UN General Assembly Annexes, Tenth Session (1955). Agenda Item 28 (Part II), p. 3.

4

The Covenants *of* Human Rights

SOME AUTHORITIES on international law claim that the Universal Declaration of 1948 is itself a compelling legal instrument. Their argument is simple. The Charter of the United Nations is a legally binding treaty. Under the Charter, all member states "pledge themselves to take joint and separate action" to promote "universal respect for, and observance of, human rights and fundamental freedoms for all without distinction as to race, sex, language or religion." Hence, insofar as the Universal Declaration specifies what men's "human rights and fundamental freedoms" are, it defines the commitments which are already made legally binding by the Covenant.*

Against this argument, however, one has to place the fact that the United Nations' own Commission on Human Rights itself has always insisted that the Declaration is "only a manifesto" and that the legally binding instrument would be the covenant, or covenants, to be completed later. The interpretation of the Universal Declaration as a statement of "ideals" was all too easily encouraged by this circumstance, as well as by the ruinously illogical overloading of the Universal Declaration with "rights" of different kinds.

International law is, in any case, much more controversial than municipal law, but insofar as it is understood to be positive law, the positivistic test of implementation and enforcement must be applied to it. It is, alas, a fact that by no means all the high contracting parties to the Charter of the United Nations have accepted Articles 55 and 56 (which commit them to uphold human rights) as having created any situation in law which did not exist before. Two examples will suffice to illustrate this.

In 1949, the Economic and Social Council of the United Nations was asked to investigate allegations of forced labor in Russia. The Soviet representative refused to consider the evidence: the allegations, he said, were propaganda "intended to divert the atten-

* See *A Standard of Achievement*, UN Publications, 58.1.22 (1958), p. 11.

The Covenants of Human Rights

tion of the working masses from their own miserable state." Neither the Soviet Union nor any other Communist government would cooperate with the United Nations by allowing an impartial commission to visit their territory to investigate the charges. The Communists took their stand on the inviolability of frontiers in international law. Subsequently a commission of inquiry, consisting of an Indian judge, a Scandinavian judge, and a South American diplomat, working in close touch with the International Labour Office, confirmed the practice of forced labor in Communist countries on the basis of the Communists' own official records. But this was as far as the United Nations could go.

Some twelve years later, in 1961, allegations of massacre by the Portuguese forces in Angola and of other abuses of human rights in South West Africa became so clamant, and were fortified with such impressive testimony from Christian missionaries and others, that the United Nations resolved once more to send an impartial commission of inquiry to investigate the situation on the spot.

Once again, the states concerned, this time Portugal and the South African Republic, brushed aside the allegations and refused to allow any United Nations commission to enter their territory, pleading the rights of sovereign states as "recognized in international law." On this occasion, the London *Times* weighed in on the side of the accused, and after observing, in a strangely frivolous phrase, that South Africa and Portugal were "on the carpet again," affirmed that the United Nations' intentions were "clearly in breach of international law" and added that the United Nations Assembly would never become effective until "respect for law becomes part of its common thinking."* This last is a high-sounding but equivocal admonition, since there are three kinds of law which the United Nations is invited by different parties to respect—municipal law, natural law, and international law, variously interpreted.

One point, at any rate, is brought home by these examples: the position of human rights is not as yet clear in international law. The proclamation of the Universal Declaration, on the understanding that it was to be followed by a legally binding instrument, in effect created a vacuum which only that legally binding instrument can fill.

Progress in this direction has, as we have seen, been slow. The Communists, who were full of warnings against things being done too quickly, have good reason for satisfaction. They have had more of their own way than they could once have allowed themselves to hope for, let alone to expect. This is not to say that the Communists have shown, in the Commission on Human Rights, much of what would generally be considered diplomatic skill. They have

---

* *The Times* (London), leading article, January 15, 1962.

The Covenants of Human Rights

been stubborn, wooden-headed, and blandly hypocritical; but the effect of this posture on the other members seems to have been curiously unnerving. A succession of *voltes-faces*, evasions, contradictions, and compromises makes up the history of Western diplomacy in the matter of human rights at the United Nations.

The purpose of the draft covenants was twofold: to set out the rights in more precise and legalistic language, and to establish machinery for implementation and enforcement.

The problem about the economic and social rights being in general unenforceable was circumvented by the device of having two covenants. There remained the question of deciding in what way the political rights were to be made positive. Some members of the Commission, not only the Communists, began at this stage to raise objections to the whole procedure. This school of thought, according to the record, complained that the setting up of international machinery for implementation "would tend to undermine the sovereignty and independence of States."

A majority of the Commission was, however, in favor of some system of implementation. There were various "proposals regarding the establishment of an international court of human rights, of *ad hoc* committees or permanent organs, which would settle disputes arising out of the interpretation or application of the covenant or otherwise supervise the observance of its provisions, and to which either states alone or individuals and groups as well as states, might submit petitions or applications."* There was, at this stage, an even division of opinion as to whether only states should have access to the proposed court, or whether petitions from individuals and non-governmental organizations should also be received.

This was noted at the Fifth Session of the Commission on Human Rights. At its Sixth Session (March to May 1950) the even division of opinion had hardened into a majority against petitions from individuals and non-governmental organizations being received. The Commission decided to recommend the setting up of a permanent juridical body, to be called the Human Rights Committee, which "would receive any complaint by any State Party to the covenant that another State Party was not giving effect to any provision thereof."†

However, at the Fifth Session of the General Assembly, held in September to December of the same year, a resolution was passed instructing the Commission on Human Rights "to proceed with the consideration of provisions to be inserted in the draft

---

* UN General Assembly Records Annexes, Tenth Session (1955). Agenda Item 28 (Part II), p. 3.
† *Ibid.*, p. 4.

The Covenants of Human Rights

covenant or separate protocols for the receipt and examination of petitions from *individuals and organizations*."*

At its next meeting, the Commission on Human Rights reaffirmed its proposal that the "measures of implementation to be included in the first draft covenant" (i.e., the one concerning political rights) "should include provisions for consideration of state-to-state complaints"; and at the same meeting, it rejected again, in the face of the General Assembly's resolution, the proposal to give the right of petition to anyone other than states. The proposal to give this right to individuals was rejected by eight votes to three, with three abstentions; and the proposal to give the right to non-governmental organizations was rejected by seven votes to four with three abstentions.†

The English-speaking delegations, which in the early days of the Commission had been so eager to establish a court to make human rights positive rights, were now on the side of circumspection. The United Nations secretariat sent out a questionnaire on the right of petition to member states, and the replies make instructive reading. Israel and the Philippines were in favor of non-governmental organizations as well as states having the right of petition, but opposed the

---
* UN General Assembly Records. Resolution 421 (V) F. [my italics].
† UN Economic and Social Council. Supplementary Vol. XI (Supp. 5, para. 37).

right being extended to individuals; Denmark proposed dealing with the problem by separate agreements; Holland and Australia thought that "for the present" only states should be admitted to the right of petition. India put forward the interesting proposal that an Attorney General or High Commissioner should be appointed to present cases to the court or committee on behalf of individuals or nongovernmental organizations. On the other hand, the United States, the United Kingdom, Norway, France, and Yugoslavia replied in favor of the right of petition being confined to states only.

Some of the governments which answered the questionnaire gave the reasons for their views. The United Kingdom argued that if the right of petition were extended to individuals, it would be abused; it would raise too many difficulties and "would place in jeopardy all the work which has been devoted" to preparing the covenants. France put forward the view that since there was not universal acceptance of the right of petition being given to individuals and unofficial bodies, it would be worse than useless to try to bring about its establishment by a majority decision. France would support it only if everybody else did.

These arguments, and others, can be found in the records of the Commission on Human Rights itself. The governments which resisted the right of individual petition made much of the consideration that the "international community was not sufficiently developed,"

The Covenants of Human Rights

and that the right of petition would be abused by frivolous, crankish, or litigious persons suffering from persecution mania. Other arguments invoked were (1) that only states could be subjects of international law; (2) that the right of petition being extended to individuals would be a threat to national sovereignty; (3) that there was no reason for doubting that states parties to the covenant would fulfill their obligations.*

Against these views, it was maintained by other members of the Commission (1) that international law is *not* concerned only with relations between states, the League of Nations' work for minorities and the Nuremberg Trials having afforded precedents of another kind; (2) that any restriction of national sovereignty arising from the covenants would be *voluntary*; (3) that all states could *not* be relied on to fulfil their obligations.†

One might have fancied that the latter was the more impressive set of arguments, but it was the former which won the day. The draft covenant on political rights which emerged from the Commission contains no fewer than fifty articles. A large proportion, namely articles 27 through 50, simply set out and delimit the powers of the Committee to be set up to sit in judgment on the petitions of states.

The earlier articles repeat, in more elaborate and at

---

* UN General Assembly Records Annexes, Tenth Session (1955). Agenda Item 28 (Part II), p. 31.
† *Loc. cit.*

the same time more guarded language, the political rights—or at any rate *some* of the political rights—named in the Universal Declaration. Article 2 obliges every contracting state to "adopt such legislation and other measures as may be necessary to give effect to the rights named in this covenant." Article 3 affirms the equality between men and women; Article 4 allows the states parties to the covenant "in time of emergency which threatens the life of the nation" to take some measures "derogating from their obligations under this covenant."

One article specifies that no one shall be arbitrarily deprived of his life; others prohibit torture and "cruel, inhuman, or degrading treatment or punishment," and forbid slavery, the slave trade, and forced labor, but specifically permit compulsory military and other national service. Another asserts that everyone has the right to liberty and security of person, and that "no one shall be deprived of his liberty except on such grounds, and in accordance with such procedure, as are established by law"; still another calls for the humane treatment of persons detained. One says that there shall be no imprisonment for breach of contract; another upholds the right of everyone to move freely within his own country and to leave any country including his own, "subject to any general law of the state concerned which provides for such reasonable restrictions as may be necessary to protect national security, public safety, health, or morals, or the rights and freedoms of others,

The Covenants *of* Human Rights

consistent with the other rights recognized by the covenant." Others forbid any expulsion of aliens except that which is "lawful"; affirm the right to a fair trial for accused persons; prohibit retroactive punishment; call for the recognition of everyone as a person before the law; and uphold the right to privacy and protection of home, correspondence, honor, and reputation.

The next group of clauses are interesting, not least for the manner in which the rights they name are limited. Article 18 affirms the right to freedom of thought, conscience, and religion "subject only to such limitations as are prescribed by law and are necessary to protect public safety, order, health, or morals, or the fundamental rights and freedom of others." Article 19 asserts the right to freedom of expression "subject to certain restrictions, but these shall be such only as are provided by law and are necessary (i) for respect of the rights or reputations of others (ii) for the protection of national security or of public order, or of public health or morals." The next two articles specify in turn the right to assembly and association, both being subject to limitations "in conformity with the law, and which are necessary in a democratic society in the interests of national security or public safety, public order, the protection of public health or morals, or the protection of the rights and freedoms of others."

The remaining articles name the right of men and women of marriageable age to marry; the right to vote and have access to the public service of one's country;

the right to equality before the law; the right of minorities to their own culture, religion, and language. Article 26 forbids the advocacy of hatred and hostility between men.

One of the rights named in the Universal Declaration does not figure in the covenant, and that is the right to property; the Commission, having failed to reach agreement on the wording, decided to adjourn the question *sine die*.* On the other hand, a right which does not appear in the Universal Declaration is set forth as Article 1 of both the covenant on political rights and that on economic and social rights. This article affirms that "all peoples and all nations have the right of self-determination," a right which is further said to "include permanent sovereignty over their natural wealth and resources." I shall return to this subject later.

I do not propose to go into details of the Commission's draft covenant on economic and social rights. I have already argued that such rights belong to a different logical category from the traditional human rights; and on the crucial issue of implementation with which I am now concerned, the draft covenant on economic and social rights offers nothing. It is not even proposed to set up a court to adjudicate on disputes between states. There is only the almost vacuous formula of "periodic reports."

---

* *Ibid.*, p. 13.

The Covenants *of* Human Rights

It should be clear so far that there is nothing very explosive in the instruments proposed. Nevertheless in 1953, when the Republican Party administration succeeded that of the Democratic Party in Washington, Mrs. Oswald B. Lord took the place of Mrs. Roosevelt as the U.S. delegate on the Commission for Human Rights and promptly announced that her government had decided not to sign any treaty on human rights drafted by the United Nations.*

In the words of Mrs. Lord's own report to the State Department:

> "The Ninth Session of the Commission on Human Rights held at Geneva from April 7 to May 30, 1953, began with an announcement by the U.S. representative that our government did not intend to sign or ratify the draft Convention on Human Rights to which the Commission had devoted its entire attention since 1948."†

Mrs. Lord's announcement came as a shock to the other non-Communist members of the Commission. To quote from a report published in *International Conciliation*, the journal of the Carnegie Endowment for International Peace:

> "The [new] position of the United States towards the covenants was deplored by several members of

* UN Document E/CN4/SR 340, May 7, 1953.
† *Bulletin* of the Department of State, Vol. XXIX, 738, August 17, 1953.

the Commission and surprise was expressed that the United States should reject covenants whose final character was as yet unknown. The Chilean delegate voiced the general reaction when he expressed 'dismay that so powerful a country as the United States should decline to assume any international legal undertaking in the sphere of human rights.' "*

The motive of the American government's *volte-face* seems to have been pressure from the right wing of the Republican Party, which feared that the draft covenants constituted a threat to national sovereignty. This fear is openly expressed in a pamphlet entitled *Human Rights and the United Nations*, published in 1952 by the Foundation for Economic Education at Irvington, New York:

> "If it [the draft covenant] is adopted, it will become the 'over law' of the adopting nations. In the case of the United States, it will become national law because the American constitution provides that a treaty adopted by the Senate shall become the supreme law of the land and the states. . . . The United Nations is attempting to control the minds of men . . . This danger is a greater threat to the citizens of the U.S.A. than any foreign military foe, for it might be that this control, together with the abrogation of the Bill of Rights, would be thrust

---
* New York, 1953, No. 493.

The Covenants *of* Human Rights

upon the American people, accomplishing by treaty that which the Constitution would prohibit being accomplished by legislation."

It was too easy for critics of the United States to suggest that the Eisenhower government was worried about its own failure to uphold the human rights named in the Universal Declaration and was afraid of having human rights enforced in America by an international agency. Mrs. Lord's announcement played nicely into the Communists' hands; it diminished the prospects of the United Nations making human rights positive rights, and it made America responsible for the damage that was done.

Time, however, changes things, if it does not always heal them. The draft covenants prepared by the Commission on Human Rights were still lingering on the agenda of the United Nations Assembly when the Republican Party administration went out of office in 1961, and Mr. Kennedy took over. Soon afterward, Mrs. Roosevelt was back at the Commission on Human Rights. Her address to the members was paraphrased as follows:

> "She had always hoped, she said, that although there were great difficulties in writing a binding treaty regarding human rights, there would some day be two treaties in both the civil and political and economic and social fields. She looked forward

to that day because then we will have made real steps forward in Human Rights."*

At the end of 1962 the draft covenants were still among business pending at the General Assembly. In the meantime, however, the Commission on Human Rights has not been entirely idle. Among other things it has been collecting information, though its success in this direction has been noticeably inhibited by its practice of seeking material only from ministerial sources. Moreover, the judicial Committee on Human Rights, as projected in the draft covenant, is to be expressly forbidden to solicit information from other quarters.

The United Nations' *Yearbook on Human Rights*, of which ten numbers have so far appeared, affords abundant evidence of the value—or futility—of official information on this subject. Each government, or each approved correspondent, contributes what it or he thinks desirable to make known about the protection of human rights in each particular country. Thus, to take, for example, the *Yearbook* for 1958, the U.S.S.R. and the other Communist countries provide particulars of the progress made in improving their people's standards of living; Italy and Japan report the closing of brothels; South Africa has a report on the Electoral Law Amendment Act of 1958, whereby "the age of 18 was substituted for the age of 21 as the age from which any

---
* UN Press Release SOC/2893, March 14, 1961. Note 2304.

The Covenants of Human Rights

white person who is a Union national . . . may be registered as a voter in elections of members of the House of Assembly and of Provincial Councils"; Spain contributes the text of the "Basic Law proclaiming the principles of the National Movement" beginning with the words, "I, Francisco Franco Bahemondo, leader of Spain, etc., etc., decree . . ." and continuing with an exposition of unadulterated fascist doctrines.

It is difficult to understand how an official United Nations publication, supposedly concerned with important developments in the direction of enlarging human rights, could thus give space to an account of a South African legal measure which is specifically and uncompromising racist (confining the vote to "any white person"); and to a Spanish fascist measure which explicitly repudiates the concept of the inalienability of the rights of man. No information whatever is given about the realities of imprisonment without trial, of arbitrary arrest, of censorship or of persecution in different countries. No one could learn the truth about "the human rights situation" from its pages.

A delegate protested mildly at the Seventeenth Session of the Commission on Human Rights that governments "appeared to have concentrated on reporting the legal, rather than the actual situation";* but the majority still resisted the idea of information being collected from unofficial sources. If the Yearbooks on

---

* UN Records E3436; E/CN4/817. Supplement 8, p. 61.

Human Rights tell the reader so little about the subject with which they are supposed to be concerned, they do throw a certain light on the narcissism of governments and the self-satisfaction of civil servants. Each has his own idea of perfection, and each is manifestly confident that his government is making rapid strides toward that noble end.

However, in February 1961 Dr. John P. Humphrey, director of the Human Rights division of the United Nations, made a speech at Wellington, New Zealand, in which he said:

> "International machinery for the protection of human rights is undoubtedly better today than it was 40 years ago, but this does not mean that human rights are necessarily better observed in practice than they were 40 years ago. It is possible that our preoccupation in the United Nations with human rights is a symptom of a gradually worsening situation. If that is so, we should probably be doing a great deal more than we are now attempting to do. But it can nevertheless be said that the United Nations is alive to the problem and that within the constitutional and other limitations we are making some contribution toward a solution of those problems and the protection of human rights."*

A "Western hemisphere seminar on human rights," organized by the United Nations in Mexico in the

---
* UN Press Release SOC/2823, February 7, 1961.

The Covenants *of* Human Rights

summer of 1961 reached an even more doleful conclusion: "On the question of the types of remedies generally available, the participants agreed that it was up to each country to develop its own institutions to make human rights effective."*

---
* UN Press Release SOC/2971, August 29, 1961.

5

Problems *of* Interpretation *and* Enforcement

I HAVE mentioned a right which appears as Article 1 of both the two draft covenants before the United Nations, but which is not named in the Universal Declaration: the right of peoples to self-determination. This was added in 1952 on a resolution of the General Assembly.

There is something peculiar about this right. All the others belong to a man in virtue of the fact that he is a man; they belong, in the language of the Universal Declaration, to "everyone," to every single individual person. Manifestly the right of "peoples" to self-determination or anything else cannot be a right in this sense. It is a collective right, the right of a society and not of an individual.

This raises immediately one of the thorniest of problems: What constitutes a "people"? Are the inhabitants of Provence or Brittany or Cornwall a people? Each is undoubtedly an ethnic group, distinguishable in many ways from the people who inhabit other parts of the political territory to which they belong. Do they have a right to self-determination which the governments of France and England should recognize? And if the answer is that there is no separatist movements among those people, what of the Welsh and the Scots and the Turkish-speaking Cypriots?

The United States government denied self-determination to the people of Virginia in the 1860's, yet the promotion of self-determination in Europe was a central aim of American policy in the First World War. The inhabitants of what became Yugoslavia and Czechoslovakia were "peoples" in American eyes; the inhabitants of Virginia were not. Likewise the United Nations, in general so zealous for self-determination, itself took up arms in 1961 against forces which claimed that the inhabitants of Katanga constitute a people.

In the case of the historic rights of man, there is no doubt about who has them. There are other difficulties of analysis, but not this one, this almost insuperable difficulty of deciding to whom the right belongs. One

Problems *of* Interpretation *and* Enforcement

might then wonder why the majority of delegates at the United Nations were so eager to put it in the covenant, and to put it, moreover, at the top of the list.

The answer lies in the strength of a certain sentiment rather than in the force of any line of reasoning. The demand for the recognition of this collective right is essentially a protest against European imperialism or colonialism. Ten years ago the membership of the United Nations was half what it is today. Then the resolution for including the right of self-determination in the covenants was supported by 36 votes to 11, with 12 abstentions. If the matter were to be voted on again in the present Assembly, the majority would certainly be much greater, for the new states which have doubled the size of the Assembly are nearly all ex-colonial territories with the very understandable desire to assert their right to their newly acquired independence and to attack the father figures of the European systems. Freedom for them is, above all, the freedom of the *nation*; and not uncommonly the freedom of the individual inhabitants of these new states has been forgotten.

It is worth noticing that the concept of the rights of peoples belongs, in the history of political thought, to that school of philosophy which is consciously at odds with the natural rights tradition; it is the Hegelian or *étatiste* rejoinder to the Stoic or liberal concept of the rights of man. It is a concept which has been nurtured especially in German minds, and is intimately linked with the German cult of the State and neglect of personal liberty. I have already mentioned that the leading German theorists of the nineteenth century asserted the rights of the German people instead of the rights of man.* This line of thinking reappears in the more sophisticated forms of fascism, for example in General Franco's "Basic Law" declaring that all other interests "must always be subordinated to the common good of the Nation."

It is thus, in a way, ironical that the anti-imperialists of the present day should invoke a concept of collective or *völkisch* right which is antithetical to personal freedom and historically allied to the most pervasive form of imperialism. One might have thought there was a world of difference between the German nationalism of the nineteenth century and the anti-colonialist nationalism of today. The German nationalists did not have to throw off any foreign yoke, but had, rather, to create a national state by the merging together of a score of separate principalities; hence the particular appeal to nineteenth-century Germans of a philosophy which recognized the "higher" freedom of the whole, that is, of the nation or the state, as opposed to the "selfish" freedom of the individual.

The newly formed republics of Africa and Asia have no need for such metaphysics. Yet in more than a few of them one can see the same process at work: a com-

---

* See "German Liberalism" in M. Cranston, *Freedom* (1953).

Problems *of* Interpretation *and* Enforcement

mon yearning for liberty is captured by movements and leaders who make the freedom of the nation from alien rule the greater part of liberty, sometimes indeed the only real liberty there is. Thus we have a situation where the freedom of the individual, the natural rights of the private person, are diminished by the very process which gives the state its freedom. Under certain forms of enlightened imperialism or alien rule, the human rights of the individuals are conspicuously *better* respected than they are by states which themselves enjoy the right of self-determination.

Compare, for example, Liberia with Hong Kong. Liberia has been an independent nation since 1847. Its very name proclaims its commitment to the ideal of freedom. Yet Liberia is a one-party state. Theoretically the people of Liberia may form other parties, and they may publish newspapers in opposition to the government. In practice the True Whig Party is a dictatorial junta. Mr. J. D. Clarke, an official of the United Nations Mission in Liberia, wrote in 1954:

> "Liberia is a police state, a one-man dictatorship in which freedom of speech is suppressed . . . The Administration is inefficient and openly corrupt . . . The small ruling class is suddenly very wealthy: the two million tribal people in the hinterland have no schools or medical services and are subject to forced labour."*

* *Manchester Guardian*, January 19, 1954.

In Hong Kong, which is one of the few remaining British colonies, the human rights and fundamental freedoms of the inhabitants are observed with such scrupulosity that even the government of China, which might claim a moral right to sovereignty over most of the populace, has not as yet ventured to attack the administration of the Governor.

Consider another example, that of British Guiana. Here, under a colonial system that has upheld the human rights and fundamental freedoms of the inhabitants, a system which was consciously designed, like British policy in West Africa and elsewere, to prepare the people for self-determination, there grew up an extreme left-wing movement, the People's Progressive Party. If the British had withdrawn from British Guiana in 1953, there is little doubt that the People's Progressive Party would have assumed total power; it had already proved itself, in free elections, the most popular party. Yet it bore a striking, or sinister, resemblance to the "popular movement" which brought Castro to power in Cuba. The people of British Guiana were probably too inexperienced in politics to realize that the People's Progressive Party could be an instrument of totalitarian rule. In the event, British "colonialism" remained as a bulwark against totalitarianism, remained as the true guardian of the people's rights and liberties; far from "promoting freedom" by quitting British Guiana, the British would in fact have been extending the range of oppression in the world.

Problems *of* Interpretation *and* Enforcement

They did so when they left Ghana to the mercies of the native dictator, Dr. Nkrumah. On the other hand, the crude, reactionary colonialism of such a government as Dr. Salazar's is as foolish as it is iniquitous.

The case of South Korea presents another melancholy spectacle. The independence and "self-determination" of this state were defended at great cost in blood by the United Nations forces (which were largely United States forces), yet the people of South Korea labor today under one of the most tyrannical governments in Asia. Instead of upholding the human rights with which the United Nations has been so much concerned, the South Korean government had reached the point in 1961 of passing the death sentence on a group of journalists—the editor and staff of *Minjok Ilbo*— for no greater crime than recommending in print some steps toward a thaw in the cold war with North Korea.*

From these illustrations it should be plain enough that the "right of peoples to self-determination" is one thing and the historic rights of man another. Indeed, if we are to seek a place where the individual's human

---

* The death sentences were passed on August 28, 1961. On November 2, 1961, the executive committee of International PEN, meeting in Rome, sent a telegram to General Chung Hi Park, Chairman of the Supreme Council in Seoul, urging him "to reconsider the *Minjok Ilbo* case and give clemency to Ji Yung Song and his colleagues." The editor of *Minjok Ilbo* was hanged, but the death sentence in the other cases was commuted to life imprisonment. The case has been the subject of representations to the government concerned both by the International PEN and by the International Press Institute.

WHAT ARE HUMAN RIGHTS?

rights have been best secured since 1945, it might well be not a sovereign state at all but one of the trust territories supervised by the United Nations.

There were originally ten trust territories; most have been absorbed in newly formed republics, though one or two remain. The interesting aspect of these territories is that the administering or "colonial" power is not entirely sovereign. It is answerable to the Trusteeship Council of the United Nations. This Council is specifically charged with protecting the human rights of the inhabitants. What is especially important is that the Council is empowered, and indeed obliged, to entertain complaints and petitions from any resident of the trust territories who feels that his human rights are being violated in any way. Several such cases have been heard and, so far as one can tell, remedied. The result of all this is that one great international lawyer, the late Sir Hirsch Lauterpächt, was able to say: "There is a wider and more explicit measure of enforcement of—some—human rights and fundamental freedoms of inhabitants of Trust Territories than in other parts of the world."*

This is not to say that all the rights named in the Universal Declaration are more fully enjoyed by the people of the Marshall Islands than they are by the people of, say, France; but the people of the Marshall Islands have one inestimable advantage over the peo-

---

* *International Law and Human Rights* (1951), p. 161.

ple of France: they have an authority beyond their own government to appeal to if they have reason to feel that any of their human rights are being taken from them or invaded.

One of the things which all the leading theorists of natural rights are agreed about is that natural rights are not absolute. Rights are founded on natural law and therefore limited by natural law. One conspicuous difference between the Universal Declaration of Human Rights and the United Nations draft covenants is that the latter attempt to name the limitations to which human rights are subject.

Thus, for example, the right of movement is limited "by such restrictions as are necessary to protect national security, public safety, health, or morals"; the right to freedom of opinion is subject to such restrictions as are "necessary to protect public safety, order, health, or morals"; the right of assembly is limited by such restrictions "as may be necessary in a democratic society in the interests of national security or public safety, public order, the protection of public health or morals."

The wording differs, in ways which may or may not be significant, as between one clause and another of the draft covenants. All clauses specify that such restrictions shall be either "prescribed by law" or be "in accordance with law."

Once again we meet some highly ambiguous concepts. First the notion of "public order" is understood quite differently in different systems of municipal law. Those responsible for drafting the covenants were, if not very good philosophers, at least lawyers enough to see this when it came to putting the text into two languages:

"The English expression 'public order' and the French expression *l'ordre public* gave rise to considerable discussion. It was observed that the English expression 'public order' was not equivalent to—and indeed was substantially different from—the French expression *l'ordre public* (or the Spanish expression *orden público*). In civil law countries, *l'ordre public* is a legal concept used principally as a basis for negating or restricting private agreements, the exercise of police power or the application of foreign law. In common law countries, the expression 'public order' is ordinarily used to mean the absence of public disorder. The common law counterpart of *l'ordre public* is 'public policy' rather than 'public order.' The use of the expression 'public order' or *l'ordre public* in the limitations clauses would create uncertainty and might constitute a basis for far-reaching derogations from the right concerned."*

Despite these considerations, the expression remains in the draft covenants. The problems it raises are, after

---

* UN General Assembly Records Annexes, Tenth Session (1955). Agenda Item 28 (Part II), p. 48.

Problems *of* Interpretation *and* Enforcement

all, no greater than those implicit in other expressions in the Covenant, and concerning which the Commission expressed no anxiety. What, for example, is to be made of that phrase which permits limitations on rights "necessary in a democratic society"? And what about the word "reasonable" in the clause which allows "reasonable" restrictions on liberties? Who is to decide what is necessary for democracy and who is to decide what is reasonable? Again, although there may be professional guidance as to what is necessary to protect public health, there are no experts on public morals.

But perhaps the most unfortunate expression of all is that which allows limitations on men's rights or liberties that are "prescribed by law" or are "in accordance with law" or "lawful." We have already noted that, so far as positive law is concerned, most invasions of men's rights and liberties *are* lawful. Only the most naive Blackstonian could find any comfort in the requirement that limitations on rights should be lawful; for it is only such as they who can go on believing that anything which is lawful must by definition be just. In their situation a dose of scepticism is a very desirable medicine.

Professor H. L. A. Hart has made this point well:

"So long as human beings can gain sufficient cooperation from some to enable them to dominate others, they will use the forms of law as one of their instruments. Wicked men will enact wicked rules which others will enforce. What surely is most needed in order to make men clear-sighted in confronting the official abuse of power is that they should preserve the sense that the certification of something as legally valid is not conclusive to the question of obedience, and that however great the aura of majesty or authority which the official system may have, its demands must in the end be submitted to moral scrutiny. This sense that there is something outside the official system, by reference to which in the last resort the individual must solve his problems of obedience, is surely more likely to be kept alive among those who are accustomed to think that rules of law may be iniquitous than among those who think that nothing iniquitous can anywhere have the status of law."*

Thus, it is not enough to say, in the words of the draft covenant, that rights may be limited by restrictions that are "lawful." In Spain, Portugal, South Africa, South Korea, and in the Communist and other states where certain human rights are limited to the point of non-existence, those restrictions are perfectly "lawful" and "valid" in positive law. What one needs to be sure of in considering restrictions on human rights is that those restrictions have the authority of natural law or morality or justice. The draft covenants of the United Nations give no indication of this crucial

---

* *The Concept of Law* (1961), pp. 205–206.

Problems *of* Interpretation *and* Enforcement

distinction between the two senses of "law," yet it is upon such a distinction that the whole reality of natural rights rests.

Once more we are led to the question of authority. Who is to decide whether the restrictions on freedom which are valid in positive law in certain places are justifiable in natural law? As things stand, every state is judge in its own cause. There is an obvious need for some impartial body to decide these things, an international court to arbitrate. But the kind of court proposed in the draft covenants, a court to which states alone shall have access, is of minimal and dubious utility. True, a dozen or more African republics would probably take up the case of the black inhabitants of South Africa. But one can think of many more instances, where no foreign power would interest itself in the fate of an individual whose rights have been invaded, and equally of instances where such a victim would not wish to have his liberty dependent on the intervention of a foreign power. There is indeed something deeply absurd in an arrangement by which something so personal and individual as the rights of man should be settled at courts to which only governments have access; it is a situation worthy of Lewis Carroll.

The United Nations is not the only international body which is interested in the protection of human rights. Another body, the Council of Europe, has already achieved something more; it has even brought into being some of those instruments for enforcement which the United Nations has contemplated and rejected.

In 1950 foreign ministers of fifteen European states signed a "European Covenant for the Protection of Human Rights and Fundamental Freedoms," and in 1952 they approved the text of a Protocol specifying three further rights. The nations represented were the United Kingdom, Belgium, Denmark, France, Western Germany, Iceland, Eire, Italy, Luxembourg, Saar, Turkey, Greece, Norway, Sweden, and Holland. Austria subscribed to the Covenant when she joined the Council of Europe in 1956.

From the beginning, the Council of Europe set itself to go forward from the enumeration of human rights to "the universal and effective recognition" of them; and the preamble to the European Covenant expressed the resolution of the High Contracting Parties "as the governments of European countries which are likeminded and have a common heritage of political traditions, ideals, freedom and the rule of law, to take the first steps for the *collective enforcement* [my italics] of certain of the rights stated in the Universal Declaration proclaimed by the United Nations in 1948."*

The specific rights the signatories agreed to protect

---

* The full text may be obtained from the Directorate of Information, Council of Europe, Strasbourg; or in Treaty Series No. 71 (1953) Cmd. 8969, from Her Majesty's Stationery Office, London.

Problems *of* Interpretation *and* Enforcement

were the historic political rights, notably the rights to life, liberty, and security of person; freedom from slavery, torture, and forced labor; the right on criminal charges to a fair and public trial; the right to privacy; freedom of thought, conscience, and religion; freedom of expression and assembly; the right to form trade unions; and the right to marry. Article 14 states:

> "The enjoyment of the rights and freedoms set forth in this Covenant shall be secured without discrimination of any ground such as sex, race, colour, language, religion, political or other opinion, national or social origin, association with a national minority, property, birth or other status."

The Protocol of 1952 gave recognition to the right of property (subject to the right of a government to impose taxes and "control the use of property as it thinks fit"); the right to education (the state "shall respect the right of parents to ensure such education and teaching in conformity with their own religious and philosophical convictions")* and the right to political suffrage (the signatories "undertake to hold free elections at reasonable intervals by secret ballot").

The importance of this European Covenant, however, lies not so much in the rights it specifies as in the fact that it contains definite legal commitments and sets up new international legal institutions.

---

* Both the United Kingdom and Greece made reservations with regard to this clause when they signed the Protocol.

The two innovations of the Council are the European Commission for Human Rights and the European Court of Human Rights. These two institutions are open to receive petitions from individuals who believe that their rights, as defined in the European Covenant, are being violated. The only proviso is that the Court shall deal only with cases which come under the jurisdiction of governments which recognize the authority of the Court. Applications from one state against another can also be entertained.

Of the two bodies, the Commission is the first to consider any petition or complaint. Its members are equal in number to that of the contracting parties. In order to prevent governments having to deal with a vast number of vexatious or unfounded petitions, the Commission has a subcommittee to weed out such cases and to conduct preliminary inquiries. When cases are accepted as *bona fide*, they are first referred to governments, and efforts are made to settle them by friendly negotiations. If these fail, the Commission has the ultimate remedy of referring the case to the European Court of Human Rights. The Commission is only partly a judicial body, having at the same time fact-finding and diplomatic duties; it also holds its meetings in private, while the European Court of Human Rights is a public court of justice in the full sense of that term. Those who sit on the Court are all professional judges; they are elected by the Consultative Assembly of the Council of Europe for a term of nine

Problems *of* Interpretation *and* Enforcement

years. The present president of the court is Lord McNair, former president of the Court of International Justice at The Hague. The other judges come from the other fourteen countries which belong to the Council of Europe. The Commission first acquired powers to consider petitions in July 1955; the Court met to hear its first case in October 1960.

The Court has so far heard two cases, one Belgian, one Irish. The reference of the Lawless case to the Commission and Court led to the release of eighty I.R.A. detainees within a week of the complaint being lodged. The appeal by De Bekker led to the Belgian government hurriedly revising its legislation about the removal of civil rights from convicted persons in such a way as to satisfy the Convention. The Commission can also claim to have contributed toward making the Cyprus settlement possible. The formal structure of both the Commission and the Court is admirable; the actual working has been radically curtailed as a result of political resistance to innovation.

In the past, international courts of justice have dealt only incidentally and peripherally with human rights. The Strasbourg Court can find some precedent in the Mixed Commission for Upper Silesia, set up by the Geneva Convention on Minorities in 1922, and in the Court of Central America. Even so, the Strasbourg Court makes legal history by the breadth of its competence, and because the Convention not only confers, through the Commission, a right of petition by individuals against their own governments but also allows, in principle, an appeal by an individual even if not a national of a member state of the Council of Europe.

Moreover, nothing exclusively "European" is claimed for the Convention. It has already been taken as a model in Africa, and its provisions have been written, by the British government, into the constitution of the new states of Nigeria, Sierra Leone, and Uganda. These provisions are being put to the test in Nigeria today. In August 1959, the foreign ministers of the Organization of American States charged their legal advisers to draft a convention incorporating, like the European Convention, a system of guarantees in the form of a commission of inquiry and a court.*

There remains a dark side to this otherwise bright picture. The great nations of Western Europe which have traditionally been the originators and custodians of the idea of rights and liberties have stood in the way of the full realization of the Council of Europe's plans. The United Kingdom has refused to recognize the jurisdiction of the European Court of Human Rights or to recognize the right of individual petition to the Commission. France has neither ratified the Convention nor recognized the jurisdiction of its legal institutions. Greece, Italy, and Turkey have taken the same line as the United Kingdom.

---

* *The Rights of the European Citizen*, with a preface by Lord McNair (Strasbourg, the Council of Europe, 1961), p. 23.

Problems *of* Interpretation *and* Enforcement

One can understand why Greece, with its hundreds of political prisoners, should hold back; but Britain, America, and France have contributed so much to the theory and tradition of human rights, have given so prominent a leadership in the international formulation of human rights, that it must seem paradoxical that they, of all nations, should hold up or stand in the way of international enforcement. A British judge, Lord McNair, is president of the European Court of Human Rights; another British jurist, Sir Humphrey Waldock, is president of the European Commission of Human Rights. All this makes it the more odd that Britain should deny the right of individual petition and withhold recognition of the Court.

The Council of Europe is in many ways, unlike the United Nations (*"ce machin"* to General de Gaulle), a French creation; it has its meeting place on French soil at Strasbourg, which makes it all the more inexplicable that France should fail to ratify the European Convention of Human Rights. Of America's policy, blowing alternately hot and cold at the United Nations on the subject of human rights, I have already spoken.

What hinders these great powers? Why, when it comes to the point, do they cling to every inch of their national sovereignty with the same grim determination with which the Communist republics cling to theirs? What, if we are to give voice to an inescapable suspicion, are they afraid of?

WHAT ARE HUMAN RIGHTS?

The position of France is, in many ways, more straightforward than that of the others. The prolonged war in Algeria created problems grave enough to justify some inroads into personal rights and liberties that would not be justifiable in ordinary times. Whether the French government has made the *kind* of inroads into civil liberties that the situation might justify is another question.

However, if France has had to face a crisis which makes shifts and compromises more intelligible than would otherwise be the case, neither America nor Britain has had such problems. Yet both these countries betray as much nervousness as France when it comes to making universal human rights universal positive rights. So far as their domestic policies are concerned, both countries have done much to extend the rights of their citizens since the Second Word War. Washington in particular has made sincere—if sometimes fruitless—efforts to protect the human rights of the Negro people in the Southern states by federal action against reactionary authorities in the states themselves.

But if these two great powers have shown a genuine concern for human rights in their recent domestic history, both are linked by deep and complex relationships with governments which do *not* respect human rights as they do themselves. In the preface to his book *Persecution 1961*, a study of the cases of nine individuals imprisoned for political reasons by governments

Problems *of* Interpretation *and* Enforcement
on both sides of the Iron Curtain, Mr. Peter Benenson wrote with regard to his two "Western" cases:

> "Antonio Amat and Agostinho Neto come from the western hemisphere. The former has a white skin and speaks Spanish; the latter is black-skinned and a well-known poet in the Portuguese tongue. Both live under *régimes* where the press and literary expression are severely censored. Those *régimes* maintain their power not so much by popular will as by political repression. Were it not for the fact that these *régimes* have buttressed their position by military alliances, in particular by granting bases for nuclear bombers, it is doubtful whether they could continue to exist. If the United States were to demonstrate the same opposition to tyranny in Spain and in Portugal as she has recently shown towards Cuba, there would be swift changes in both countries—and freedom for these men, and for many thousands like them."*

If the United States is thus sustaining Iberian oppression, the United Kingdom is even more closely linked with governments which show the same disregard for human rights. For whatever it is which still unifies the British Commonwealth also ties Britain to such *régimes* as that in Ghana, where hundreds of people ill-regarded by Dr. Nkrumah are kept in

---

* *Persecution, 1961* (1961), pp. 10–11.

prison without trial; and ties Britain still more closely to the various white *régimes* in Southern and Central Africa which are openly and unashamedly committed to policies of racial discrimination.

Of course we cannot expect that men's moral rights shall be the same in all places and at all times. There is a connection between human rights being universal and their formulation being generalized and wide. The basic general principles of morality are minimal precisely because they are universal. Human rights rest on universal principles, but the precise moral rights of men in some communities differ from the precise moral rights of men in other communities, and this is one reason why the formulation of human rights cannot be at the same time closely detailed and of universal application. The moral rights of Englishmen today are not exactly what they were in 1688. Today it is generally agreed in England that the right to liberty entails the right of every adult person to a vote. The right to liberty was not seen in this way in 1688, for then the great illiterate mass of Englishmen neither understood elections nor felt the lack of a vote as a limitation on their freedom.

Similarly today in Switzerland—commonly regarded as one of the most free and most democratic countries —the women have no vote; but so long as the women do not *want* to vote and are content with the ancient institution of household suffrage—are content, that is to say, to allow their husbands and fathers to vote

Problems *of* Interpretation *and* Enforcement

in their name—then we cannot say that a natural right is being denied to the women of Switzerland. A right presupposes a claim; if the claim is not made, the question of a right does not arise.

But once the claim *is* made, the situation is altered. Lauterpächt once wrote of human rights: "Inasmuch as, upon final analysis, they are an expression of moral claims, they are a powerful lever of legal reform. The moral claims of today are often the legal rights of tomorrow."*

In the advanced, industrialized societies of Europe and North America the claims that are made, and can be reasonably made, by the whole body of inhabitants are considerably greater than could reasonably be made by the majority of people in Asia, Africa, and South America. With industrial progress, one passes from the minimal code of the rights of man to more elaborate rights, including the "economic and social" rights named in the Universal Declaration. But progress should not blind us to the meaning of those minimal rights, for to assert them is to say that no society is so backward that its members can justly be denied them.

I realize uneasily that to talk of some communities being more backward than others and of more advanced societies having more extended moral rights is to lay oneself open to misunderstanding. For it is

---

* *Op. cit.*, p. 74.

thus that the apologists of *apartheid* speak and the champions of crude imperialism who say that man of color can never qualify for the same moral rights as white men. But this is the opposite of truth. If one believes in moral rights at all, one cannot do less than accept Cecil Rhodes's maxim of equal rights for the equally civilized, and color is irrelevant to this criterion. One might perhaps say that the reason why the Republic of South Africa has increasingly alienated the outside world is that it has in recent years so aggressively repudiated Cecil Rhodes. What stirred the Afrikaners to evolve the policy of *apartheid* was not that the black Africans were primitive, but that the black Africans were *ceasing* to be primitive, and beginning to yield an educated class which claimed, and could reasonably claim, equality with the Europeans.

The key document in the history of *apartheid* is the Bantu Education Act, which was designed to close or nationalize the schools in which the Christian missionaries were training an educated African *élite*, and furthermore to shut the doors of the South African universities to non-European students. In the words of the Minister of Native Affairs: "There is no place for him [the black African] in the European community above the level of certain humble forms of work."*

Thus the central aim of *apartheid* is to keep the black Africans "in their place," to halt the process

---
* Quoted by Peter Abrahams, "L'Afrique et L'Occident," *Comprendre*, No. 13–14 (Venice, 1955), p. 11.

Problems *of* Interpretation *and* Enforcement

whereby they were becoming as sophisticated and advanced as the Afrikaners, to push them back into tribalism and primitivism. And this, of course, is the very reverse of that policy which has been the main moral justification for the existence of the British Empire, namely that the Empire brought backward people forward, educated, trained, and equipped them to live according to the same rule of law by which Englishmen themselves had learned to live.

If rights are to be differently understood in different places, so will there in different places be different limitations placed on the exercise of certain rights. The right to freedom of expression and action is universally limited by the rule that others shall not be injured by anyone's use of his liberty; such use, we say, becomes an "abuse" of the right to liberty.

But different people are injured by different things, and there are great differences of opinion as to what is likely to cause an injury to others. Thus, for example, the morals of the British public were held some years ago to be threatened by a novel called *The Philanderer*, which had circulated freely, and presumably harmlessly, in America, and the book was suppressed by an English Court. Nudist magazines, freely sold and considered morally wholesome in Scandinavia, have been suppressed in both England and America, on the grounds that the representation of pubic hair constitutes a moral danger to the British and American public, although nude photographs are otherwise considered harmless in those countries. In Russia and other Communist countries an even more markedly Victorian view is taken of the moral danger to society contained in erotic art and literature.

Censorship of one kind or another is perhaps inevitable in any society, and no philosopher has yet worked out a really satisfactory formula for a policy of toleration. John Stuart Mill believed that the state and society should tolerate all "self-regarding actions," all actions which affected no one injuriously beside the agent; but Mill himself, when challenged, was hard pressed to find examples of such actions, since almost everything we do affects other people somehow, and no one can say with certainty how harmless or how injurious these effects are going to be.

But this is not to say that we cannot distinguish between one kind of censorship and another. It would be a great mistake, for example, to equate the British suppression of *The Philanderer* with the Russian suppression of *Dr. Zhivago*. For whatever one's view of what does or does not jeopardize the moral welfare of society, the defense of moral welfare is a very different objective from the defense of a particular political system or *régime*. *Dr. Zhivago* was not suppressed in Russia to protect the public; it was suppressed to protect the government and the system. The right to free speech gives one no right to injure one's neighbor,

Problems *of* Interpretation *and* Enforcement

morally or physically; but it does give one an unambiguous right to criticize one's ruler and the ideology on which that rule is based. If censorship can be invoked, justifiably, to protect the innocent from corruption, that is not to say it can be invoked to protect statesmen and politicians from criticism.

An analysis of the limitations which may be placed on human rights is thus as important as an analysis of the rights themselves; otherwise muddle-headed claims for rights are countered by equally muddle-headed arguments about the needs of public order and security. Reason, in this as in other things, is not a bad guide to go by. For example, it is reasonable in many societies to limit the right to marry to persons over sixteen, since this limitation on the right can serve to protect children from injury; but it can never be reasonable to forbid people to marry persons of another race or color (as is now the law in South Africa), since such marriages can do no conceivable harm to anyone. It is reasonable that clubs should exclude candidates disliked by their members, for this is part of the right of privacy; but it is not reasonable that public institutions such as hotels should have a general rule excluding persons of any race.

If the American government has reason to believe that the free movement of members of the Communist Party constitutes a threat to national security, then that government may have a *prima facie* case for impounding passports; but the South African government's refusal of passports to black African scholars, on the sole grounds that such scholars are black, has no case in reason whatever.

Even so, I think too much is made of the supposed antithesis between security and freedom. A few years ago in London an all-party Conference of Privy Councillors on Security agreed that "it is right to continue the practice of tilting the balance in favour of offering greater protection to the security of the state rather than in the direction of safeguarding the rights of the individual." Now this, if it meant what it seems to mean, would be one of the most alarming utterances to have issued from an all-party committee in England in peace time. In fact, it was intended to mean something fairly unsensational. The Privy Councillors at this conference were dealing with spying, notably with spying in the civil service, and the principle they were laying down was that in borderline cases where a civil servant is thought to have Communist attachments, the traditional rights of the individual civil servant should not be upheld at the risk or expense of state security. The conference was an aftermath of the Burgess and Maclean case, and a certain amount of fussy locking of the stable door was only to be expected.

Personally I should not quarrel with the verdict of the conference insofar as it concerns the conditions of employment in the civil service. Locke, for one, always maintained that toleration could not be extended to people with a loyalty to a foreign power; and it may be

Problems *of* Interpretation *and* Enforcement

only sensible that certain public offices should be closed to members of a party which puts loyalty to Russia above loyalty to one's native country. But the wording of the Privy Councillors' statement is such that it may easily be read as authorizing something far greater than this. If what was intended as a working rule to be followed in counter-espionage tribunals were taken as a general principle of government policy, then it would be truly ominous.

And what makes it so ominous is that phrase about "tilting the balance" in favor of state security "rather than in the direction of safeguarding the rights of the individual." For this image of a balance is something alien to the whole idea of the rights of man—alien, for that matter, to the central political beliefs of Western democracy. The balance suggests that the more you push down one side, the side of individual rights, the more the other side, the side of state security, will rise. Now it is true that the promotion of state security does entail some small diminution of individual freedom, but from this it does not follow that the less liberty you have the more security you have, or that any increase in security must bring a corresponding reduction of freedom.

In the English-speaking world, ordinary people for generations have maintained that the abridgment of individual rights beyond a certain small degree would not only *not* promote the security of the state but would positively *jeopardize* the security of the state. Popular scorn for foreign tyrants is not only a matter

WHAT ARE HUMAN RIGHTS?

of disapproval; it stems also from a sense of the folly of the foreign tyrant's notion that security can be gained by the repression of liberty. To such eyes the present government of Portugal looks vastly more precarious than, say, the present government of Norway.

To claim the rights of man is to claim, among other things, both security *and* liberty. Security is not something which is antithetical to human rights, because security is itself a human right. The security of the individual is bound up with the security of the community; the private enjoyment of a right is bound up with the common enjoyment of the right. The demand for liberty and security is not the demand for two things which can only with difficulty be balanced or reconciled; it is the demand for two things which naturally belong together.

Part of what is meant by the traditional Western faith in freedom is the belief that a free country is *safer* than an unfree country. I think there are good grounds for continuing to believe that this is true. But beyond this historical generalization there is that other principle which is even more important—the moral judgment, the ultimate decision that an unfree society is an intolerable society and that even if some sort of security could be bought at the cost of liberty or any other fundamental human right, that security would not be worth having and life in such a political society would not be worth living.

Appendix

Text of the Universal Declaration of Human Rights proclaimed by the General Assembly of the United Nations, December 1948

PREAMBLE

W<small>HEREAS</small> recognition of the inherent dignity and of the equal and inalienable rights of all members of the human family is the foundation of freedom, justice and peace in the world,

W<small>HEREAS</small> disregard and contempt for human rights have resulted in barbarous acts which have outraged the conscience of mankind, and the advent of a world in which human beings shall enjoy freedom of speech and belief and freedom from fear and want has been proclaimed as the highest aspiration of the common people,

WHEREAS it is essential, if man is not to be compelled to have recourse, as a last resort, to rebellion against tyranny and oppression, that human rights should be protected by the rule of law,

WHEREAS it is essential to promote the development of friendly relations between nations,

WHEREAS the peoples of the United Nations have in the Charter reaffirmed their faith in fundamental human rights, in the dignity and worth of the human person and in the equal rights of men and women and have determined to promote social progress and better standards of life in larger freedom,

WHEREAS Member States have pledged themselves to achieve, in co-operation with the United Nations, the promotion of universal respect for and observation of human rights and fundamental freedoms,

WHEREAS a common understanding of these rights and freedoms is of the greatest importance for the full realisation of this pledge,

NOW, THEREFORE, THE GENERAL ASSEMBLY proclaims

THIS UNIVERSAL DECLARATION OF HUMAN RIGHTS as a common standard of achievement for all peoples and all nations, to the end that every indi-

Appendix

vidual and every organ of society, keeping this Declaration constantly in mind, shall strive by teaching and education to promote respect for these rights and freedoms and by progressive measures, national and international, to secure their universal and effective recognition and observance, both among the peoples of Member States themselves and among the peoples of territories under their jurisdiction.

Article 1. All human beings are born free and equal in dignity and rights. They are endowed with reason and conscience and should act towards one another in a spirit of brotherhood.

Article 2. Everyone is entitled to all the rights and freedoms set forth in this Declaration, without distinction of any kind, such as race, colour, sex, language, religion, political or other opinion, national or social origin, property, birth or other status.

Furthermore, no distinction shall be made on the basis of the political, jurisdictional or international status of the country or territory to which a person belongs, whether it be independent, trust, non-self-governing or under any other limitation of sovereignty.

Article 3. Everyone has the right to life, liberty, and security of person.

Article 4. No one shall be held in slavery or servitude; slavery and the slave trade shall be prohibited in all their forms.

Article 5. No one shall be subjected to torture or to cruel, inhuman or degrading treatment or punishment.

Article 6. Everyone has the right to recognition everywhere as a person before the law.

Article 7. All are equal before the law and are entitled without any discrimination to equal protection of the law. All are entitled to equal protection against any discrimination in violation of this Declaration and against any incitement to such discrimination.

Article 8. Everyone has the right to an effective remedy by the competent national tribunals for acts violating the fundamental rights granted him by the constitution or by law.

Article 9. No one shall be subject to arbitrary arrest, detention or exile.

Article 10. Everyone is entitled in full equality to a fair and public hearing by an independent and impartial tribunal, in the determination of his rights and obligations and of any criminal charge against him.

Appendix

Article 11. (1) Everyone charged with a penal offence has the right to be presumed innocent until proved guilty according to law in a public trial at which he has had all the guarantees necessary for his defence.

(2) No one shall be held guilty of any penal offence on account of any act or omission which did not constitute a penal offence, under national or international law, at the time when it was committed. Nor shall a heavier penalty be imposed than the one that was applicable at the time the penal offence was committed.

Article 12. No one shall be subjected to arbitrary interference with his privacy, family, home or correspondence, nor to attacks upon his honour and reputation. Everyone has the right to the protection of the law against such interference or attacks.

Article 13. (1) Everyone has the right to freedom of movement and residence within the borders of each State.

(2) Everyone has the right to leave any country, including his own, and to return to his country.

Article 14. (1) Everyone has the right to seek and to enjoy another country's asylum from persecution.

(2) This right may not be invoked in the case of prosecutions genuinely arising from non-political

crimes or from acts contrary to the purposes and principles of the United Nations.

Article 15. (1) Everyone has the right to a nationality.

(2) No one shall be arbitrarily deprived of his nationality nor denied the right to change his nationality.

Article 16. (1) Men and women of full age, without any limitation due to race, nationality or religion, have the right to marry and to found a family. They are entitled to equal rights as to marriage, during marriage and at its dissolution.

(2) Marriage shall be entered into only with the free and full consent of the intending spouses.

(3) The family is the natural and fundamental group unit of society and is entitled to protection by society and the State.

Article 17. (1) Everyone has the right to own property alone as well as in association with others.

(2) No one shall be arbitrarily deprived of his property.

Article 18. Everyone has the right to freedom of thought, conscience and religion; this right includes freedom to change his religion or belief, and freedom, either alone or in community with others, and in public or private, to manifest his religion or belief in teaching, practice, worship and observance.

Article 19. Everyone has the right to freedom of opinion and expression; this right includes freedom to hold opinions without interference and to seek, receive, and impart information and ideas through any media and regardless of frontiers.

Article 20. (1) Everyone has the right to freedom of peaceful assembly and association.

(2) No one may be compelled to belong to an association.

Article 21. (1) Everyone has the right to take part in the government of his country, directly or through freely chosen representatives.

(2) The will of the people shall be the basis of the authority of government; this will shall be expressed in periodic and genuine elections which shall be by universal and equal suffrage and shall be held by secret vote or by equivalent free voting procedures.

Article 22. Everyone, as a member of society, has the right to social security and is entitled to realisation, through national effort and international cooperation and in accordance with the organisation and resources of each State, of the economic, social and cultural rights indispensable for his dignity and the free development of his personality.

Article 23. (1) Everyone has the right to work, to free choice of employment, to just and favorable conditions of work, and to protection against unemployment.

(2) Everyone, without any discrimination, has the right to equal pay for equal work.

(3) Everyone who works has the right to just and favorable remuneration ensuring for himself and his family an existence worthy of human dignity, and supplemented, if necessary, by other means of social protection.

(4) Everyone has the right to form and to join trade unions for the protection of his interests.

Article 24. Everyone has the right to rest and leisure, including reasonable limitation of working hours and periodic holidays with pay.

Article 25. (1) Everyone has the right to a standard of living adequate for the health and well-being of himself and of his family, including food, clothing, housing and medical care and necessary social services, and the right to security in the event of unemployment, sickness, disability, widowhood, old age or other lack of livelihood in circumstances beyond his control.

(2) Motherhood and childhood are entitled to special care and assistance. All children, whether born in or out of wedlock, shall enjoy the same social protection.

Article 26. (1) Everyone has the right to education. Education shall be free, at least in the elementary and fundamental stages. Elementary education shall be compulsory. Technical and professional education shall be made generally available and higher education shall be equally accessible to all on the basis of merit.

(2) Education shall be directed to the full development of the human personality and to the strengthening of respect for human rights and fundamental freedoms. It shall promote understanding, tolerance and friendship among all nations, racial or religious groups, and shall further the activities of the United Nations for the maintenance of peace.

(3) Parents have a prior right to choose the kind of education that shall be given to their children.

Article 27. (1) Everyone has the right freely to participate in the cultural life of the community, to enjoy the arts and to share in scientific advancement and its benefits.

(2) Everyone has the right to the protection of the moral and material interests resulting from any scientific, literary or artistic production of which he is the author.

Article 28. Everyone is entitled to a social and international order in which the rights and freedoms set forth in this Declaration can be fully realized.

Article 29. (1) Everyone has duties to the community in which alone the free and full development of his personality is possible.

(2) In the exercise of his rights and freedoms, everyone shall be subject only to such limitations as are determined by law solely for the purpose of securing due recognition and respect for the rights and freedoms of others and of meeting the just requirements of morality, public order and the general welfare in a democratic society.

(3) These rights and freedoms may in no case be exercised contrary to the purposes and principles of the United Nations.

Article 30. Nothing in this Declaration may be interpreted as implying for any State, group or person any right to engage in any activity or to perform any act aimed at the destruction of any of the rights and freedoms set forth herein.

Short Bibliography

S. BENN and R. S. PETERS, *Social Principles and the Democratic State* (1959).

I. BERLIN, *Two Concepts of Liberty* (1958).

J. L. BRIERLY, *The Law of Nations* (1955).

J. L. BRIERLY, *The Basis of Obligation in International Law* (1958).

R. K. CARR (ed.), "Civil Rights in America," *Annals of the American Academy of Political and Social Science*, May, 1951.

M. R. COHEN, *Reason and Law* (1931).

M. CRANSTON, *Freedom* (1953).

A. P. D'ENTRÈVES, *Natural Law* (1951).

G. G. FITZMAURICE, "The Foundations of the Authority of International Law," *Modern Law Review*, No, 19, 1956.

J. FRANK, *Law and the Modern Mind* (1949).

W. FRIEDMANN, *Law in a Changing Society* (1958).

L. L. FULLER, "American Legal Philosophy in Mid-Century," *Journal of Legal Education*, 1954.

C. G. HAINES, *The Revival of Natural Law Concepts* (1930).

J. HALL, "Concerning the Nature of Positive Law," *Yale Law Journal*, 1949.

C. J. HAMSON, *The Law: Its Study and Comparison* (1950).
G. T. HANKIN, *Human Rights* (1951).
H. L. A. HART, "Philosophy of Law and Jurisprudence," *Britain-American Journal of Comparative Law*, 1953.
H. L. A. HART, "Theory and Definition in Jurisprudence," *Proceedings of the Aristotelian Society*, Supp., Vol. 29, 1955.
H. L. A. HART, *The Concept of Law* (1961).
A. N. HOLCOMBE, *Human Rights in the Modern World* (1948).
The Human Rights Yearbooks (United Nations, New York).
P. IGÑOTUS, *Political Prisoner* (1959).
P. C. JESSUP, "The Reality of International Law," *Foreign Affairs*, No. 118, 1940.
H. KANTOROWICZ, *The Definition of Law* (1958).
E. KEDOURIE, *Nationalism* (1960).
E. N. VAN KLEFFENS, "Sovereignty and International Law," *Recueil des Cours*, Vol. 1, 1953.
H. KOROWICZ, "The Problem of the International Personality of Individuals," *American Journal of International Law*, Vol. 50, 1956.
P. LASLETT (ed.), *Philosophy, Politics and Society* (1956).
H. LAUTERPÄCHT, *International Law and Human Rights* (1951).
A. B. McNULTY and M. A. EISSEN, "The European Commission of Human Rights," *Journal of the International Commission of Jurists*, Vol. 1, No. 2.
J. MARITAIN, *The Rights of Man* (1944).
J. MARITAIN (ed.), *Human Rights: Comments and Interpretations* (1950).
G. MARSHALL, "Law in a Cold Climate," *Juridical Review*, 1956.
A. MARTIN, "Human Rights and World Politics," *Yearbook of World Affairs*, 1951.
A. MELDEN (ed.), *Essays in Moral Philosophy* (1958).

Short Bibliography

W. L. MORISON, "Some Myths About Positivism," *Yale Law Journal*, 1958.

D. P. MYERS, "Human Rights in Europe," *American Journal of International Law*, Vol. 48, 1954.

D. P. MYERS, "The European Commission on Human Rights," *American Journal of International Law*, Vol. 50, 1956.

M. OAKESHOTT, "The Concept of a Philosophical Jurisprudence," *Politics*, 1937–38.

K. OLIVEKRONA, *Law as Fact* (1939).

J. PLAMENATZ, *On Alien Rule and Self-Government* (1961).

J. PLAMENATZ, *Consent, Freedom and Political Obligation* (1938).

M. RADIN, "Natural Law and Natural Rights," *Yale Law Journal*, 1950.

D. D. RAPHAEL, "Law and Morals," *Philosophical Quarterly*, 1954.

D. G. RITCHIE, *Natural Rights* (1895).

A. H. ROBERTSON, *The Council of Europe* (1956).

A. H. ROBERTSON, "The European Court of Human Rights," *International and Comparative Law Quarterly*, April, 1959.

S. M. SCHWEBEL, *The Secretary-General of the United Nations* (1952).

G. L. WILLIAMS, "Language and the Law," *Law Quarterly Review*, 1945–46.

R. WOLLHEIM, "The Nature of Law," *Political Studies*, No. 2, 1954.

The Yearbooks of the European Commission of Human Rights (The Hague, 1955).

DATE DUE

MAY 2 3 2004		

GAYLORD   PRINTED IN U.S.A.